ANTI-SUFFRAGE ESSAYS

LECTOR HOUSE PUBLIC DOMAIN WORKS

ANTI-SUFFRAGE ESSAYS

VARIOUS,
ERNEST BERNBAUM

ISBN: 978-93-90015-77-1

Published: 1916

LECTOR HOUSE LLP
E-MAIL: lectorpublishing@gmail.com

ANTI-SUFFRAGE ESSAYS

BY

MASSACHUSETTS WOMEN

WITH AN INTRODUCTION
BY
ERNEST BERNBAUM, PH.D.
(HARVARD UNIVERSITY)

1916

CONTENTS

INTRODUCTION

THE ANTI-SUFFRAGE VICTORY IN MASSACHU-SETTS

The essays in this little book are by anti-suffrage women who were prominent speakers, writers, and organizers, in the campaign of 1915. They voice sentiments which gained the largest measure of popular support ever accorded in the history of Massachusetts politics.

The largest number of votes any political party polled in Massachusetts before 1915 was 278,976. The anti-suffragists polled 295,939. Since 1896 there has been but one instance in which the voters gained a plurality amounting to 110,000 votes. The anti-suffragists won by 133,447 votes. Alton B. Parker's defeat by Theodore Roosevelt in 1904 is commonly regarded as typifying political annihilation; but the suffragists in 1915 did not poll as many votes as Mr. Parker, and the anti-suffragists polled 38,000 more than President Roosevelt at the height of his popularity. Such outworn words as "overwhelming" and "landslide," which have been regularly used to describe victories not half so great as this, understate the actual extent of the anti-suffrage triumph. The pronounced aversion which Massachusetts showed towards Horace Greeley in the presidential campaign of 1872, and towards William J. Bryan in that of 1896, scarcely exceeded that which she feels towards the suffragists today.

The grounds of this aversion are so numerous that it is difficult to determine which of the many causes of the anti-suffrage victory were the most powerful. In my opinion, however, Massachusetts men defeated woman suffrage chiefly because (1) they discovered that nine women out of ten did not want to vote; (2) they knew that the creation of a large body of stay-at-home voters would result in bad government; and (3) they grew disgusted with the temperament, the notions, and the methods typical of the few women who clamored for the vote.

For at least two generations suffragists have been spending a huge amount of energy and money in spreading their doctrine. Contributions, mainly drawn from a few rich women, have enabled them to send professional speakers into every district of the state, to distribute tons of "literature," to supply the press with a constant stream of "news" written from their point of view, and in general to advertise their claims in the most lavish way. A propaganda so subsidized would have been successful decades ago if sound principles and common sense were on its side. But to their consternation the suffragists found that the vast majority of Massachusetts women turned a deaf ear to their plausible appeals, and that their strongest opponents were those of their own sex.

Suffragists continued to talk about what "we women" want. But men presently began to see that these women had no right to pretend to represent their sex. Even their own claims as to the number of women supporting them showed that they represented only between 5% and 10% of the women of Massachusetts. At least 90% of the women—either by open opposition, or by a marked indifference to the subject—showed that they did not believe in woman suffrage. It became obvious that no general statement could be more emphatically true than that Massachusetts women did not want to vote.

When this truth was insistently pressed upon the suffragists, they were apt to call the indifferent women "unenlightened." This was felt to be an insult rather than an explanation. The average Massachusetts man does not think his mother, wife, and sister "unenlightened"—certainly not on the suffrage question. She has heard and read the suffrage notions again and again. He knows that if she felt that man was her oppressor, or that the welfare of herself or her family would be increased by her enfranchisement, she would say so. She is a sensible, observant woman, who knows what she wants, does not hesitate to ask for it, and usually gets it. But she was not asking for the ballot. It did not take her long to see through the suffrage fallacy that "only those women would need to vote who want to." She realized that the vote would mean an obligation as well as a privilege, and that she could not honorably accept the privilege without undertaking the obligation. Her life being already crowded with duties that only she could discharge, she would not add to them one that her husband, brother, or son can discharge at least as well.

If any man wondered whether his personal inquiries among the women of his acquaintance gave a sufficiently broad basis for the belief that women did not want to vote, he became convinced of the fact when he learned about the Drury bill of 1913. This bill would have given Massachusetts women a chance to vote "Yes" or "No" on woman suffrage. The proposal resulted in the amazing revelation that the suffragists were afraid to let women vote on the question. They worked against the bill because they knew that an official count would disclose how pitiably small a fraction of women were on their side. They thought that their little group, by noisy publicity, could be made to appear a considerable number. But the men, when they discovered who opposed the Drury bill, were not deceived. They saw that a small minority of women was trying to induce them to coerce the great majority. They awoke to the fact that the suffragist's demand was not that men should grant women an expressed desire, but that men, contemptuously disregarding the evident wishes of women, should force upon them a heavy responsibility.

The nature of that responsibility brings us to what seems to me the second important cause for the suffrage defeat. Men—more than politically inexperienced women,—know that good government depends upon the willingness of the electorate to do its duty vigilantly and regularly. The greatest good of the greatest number of classes (including the women and children in each class) can be secured only when a large proportion of the eligible voters vote. Those voters who are led by bosses, or by selfish interests, go to the polls steadily. Their influence can be offset only when the rest of the electorate goes likewise. The results of elections in which a small proportion of the eligible voters take part, are poor laws and incompetent or corrupt government. The leading political issues—the tariff, trusts, transportation, military and police force, taxation, finance, etc.—bear directly upon the work of men in their trades and business, and under male suffrage a fairly large proportion of the vote is cast. The life-work of women removes them from contact with these political questions, and the nature of most women is not attracted by the contentious spirit in which political warfare is conducted. As long as no more than 10% of the women took an interest in the woman suffrage question itself, no man could reasonably expect them to be otherwise than indifferent to the regular subjects of political conflict. To impose political duties upon the sex against its will was simply to create conditions that encouraged corrupt and feeble government. The soundness of this principle was, furthermore, being demonstrated in woman-suffrage territory, such cities as Seattle and such states as Colorado showing that sooner or later a neglectful electorate leads to the downfall of good government.

The third cause for the defeat of woman suffrage was the disgust which the manners, methods, and unethical sentiments of the suffragists aroused. This is not pleasant to dwell upon, but was too important an influence in the campaign to leave unmentioned. The suffragists professed to "occupy higher moral ground," to uplift politics, and to elevate womanhood. The longer one observed their deeds and words, the surer one became that they were not uplifting politics and that they tended to disgrace women in men's eyes. The tone of politics can be improved if the contestants will avoid false assertions and unnecessary personal attacks. The suffragists said and did things which were, like militancy, excusable only on the immoral ground that the end justifies the means.

As an example of their disingenuous statements, the following may serve. The National Woman Suffrage Association circulated a flyer entitled "Twenty Facts About Woman Suffrage." "Fact No. 15," under the heading, "How Women Vote," read: "Arizona, California, Colorado and Washington are the only states in the Union which have eight-hour laws for working women." Any unsuspecting reader would infer just what he was intended to infer—namely, that it was woman suffrage that brought about all these eight-hour laws, and that male suffrage had not brought about any of them. A more nearly truthful heading for this "fact" would have been "How Men Vote." The credit for passing the eight-hour law in California and in Washington (also in Arizona so far as laundry workers are concerned) belongs to legislatures elected by men alone. False suggestions of this type no doubt gained many proselytes in parlor meetings; but when they were made in the open forum of a public campaign, their untruth was exposed, and the voters grew indignant that women should thus have tried to mislead them. The suffragists only made a bad matter worse by alleging that their anti-suffrage sisters were given to misrepresentations and to every other crime in the political calendar; for men thereupon concluded that if this initial participation in politics had such a demoralizing effect on the women of each side, it was best to keep both parties out of the arena altogether.

The suffragists' tendencies to make bitter personal attacks was repeatedly shown. Not wishing to resurrect some of the venomous charges brought against anti-suffrage women, I take leave to illustrate the baseless characters of such attacks by one made against myself. In the spring of 1915, I gave a series of lectures on the fundamental principles of anti-suffrage. The audiences were gratifyingly large; there was a demand for several repetitions of the lectures; and, apparently, the suffragists felt that something must be done to destroy my pernicious influence. Instead of answering my arguments, the President of the Massachusetts Suffrage Association, Miss Alice Stone Blackwell, wrote an editorial in her "Woman's Journal," saying:

"This young gentleman is a Dane, and he has been very fluent and somewhat contemptuous in giving reasons why American women should not be allowed to vote."

The statement was, as usual, spread broadcast through the suffrage columns of the Massachusetts newspapers; and doubtless my opponents indulged the hope that in the wave of national feeling which was then beginning to rise, anybody thus branded as a foreigner would be badly discredited. As a matter of fact, I was born in Brooklyn, N. Y. (If I had chosen to imitate Miss Blackwell's method of controversy, I might have retorted that my father, who was born in Denmark, but who came to America in 1855, fought as a volunteer officer in the Navy of the United States in the Civil War, at a time when Miss Blackwell's father was engaged in a safer occupation.)

The repellant impression made upon men by the suffragists' misstatements and personal abusiveness was deepened by their support of militancy and feminism. As to the unethical character of the latter, Mrs. Foxcroft's essay in this book presents startling and irrefutable testimony. As to militancy, it may be said that this furnished the most glaring (though not the only) evidence of the evil effect of political activity on women. Much is usually made of the fact that Mrs. Pankhurst and her accomplices in crime destroyed a large amount of valuable property. But the greatest injury she and her American idolizers did was to lower man's ideal of woman. They tried to make the virago a heroine. They did not succeed; but the more Mrs. Pankhurst's apologists glorified her, the more men were determined not to endorse a party that tempted women to abandon real womanliness for mock masculinity.

ERNEST BERNBAUM

CAMBRIDGE, MASS.
February, 1916

N. B.—

To prevent misunderstanding, it should be said that though the following essays represent in general the views of Massachusetts anti-suffragists, the responsibility for the facts and opinions given in the various essays rests with the individual writers alone.

ANTI-SUFFRAGE ESSAYS

WHO THE MASSACHUSETTS ANTI-SUF-FRAGISTS ARE

MRS. JOHN BALCH

Katharine Torbert Balch, wife of John Balch; Treasurer of the Summer Industrial School of Milton; member of the Executive Committee of the Milton Branch of the Civil Service Reform Association; director of the Ely Club of New York City; member of the Executive Committee of the special Preparedness Committee appointed by Governor Walsh; President of the Massachusetts Women's Anti-Suffrage Association.

J. A. H.

In reply to oft-repeated calumnies about the membership and affiliations of the Anti-Suffrage Association, I offer a plain statement of facts which can be verified.

36,761 Massachusetts women, twenty-one years of age or over, are to-day registered members of the Massachusetts Women's Anti-Suffrage Association. They are not confined to one section of the state, but are found distributed among no less than 443 cities, towns, and villages. Each year the organization increases; and each year the members of the 137 state branches draw closer together in their opposition to suffrage and their striving for the true progress of woman and of civilization.

These women are not of only one class or type. An examination of our enrollment reveals among our members not only the very large group of homemakers, but also authors, doctors, lawyers, teachers, librarians, newspaper-writers, stenographers, social service workers, cooks, housemaids, nurses, milliners, insurance agents, restaurant-keepers, clerks, shopkeepers, private secretaries, dressmakers, seamstresses, etc., etc. During the recent campaign, the co-operation, devotion, and self-sacrifice of this body of women was inspiring. From the wage-earner who endured systematic nagging, if not persecution, from suffragists, to the woman of wealth who gave of her vitality to the breaking point, daily came the evidences of immovable faith in the righteousness of their cause.

Many of our leaders are prominent in public welfare activities. The late Mrs. Charles D. Homans, one of the founders of our organization, was an active and important member of the Massachusetts Prison Commission. Mrs. James M. Codman, our beloved ex-President, has served twenty years on the State Board of Charities, was one of the first women overseers of the poor ever elected in this state, and has long been one of the managers of a large private hospital. Miss Mary S. Ames, a former President, is a member of the Executive Council (New England section) of the National Civic Federation, Chairman of the Committee on Practical Training for Girls, a Trustee of the Boston Home for Incurables, one of the managers of the Women's Free Hospital, a director of the Brook House Home for Working Girls, a member of the Easton Agricultural Vocational Training Committee, a Trustee of Unity Church (Easton), and a member of the Advisory Board of the Belgian Relief Committee. Mrs. Henry P. Kidder, of our Executive Board, is President of the Woman's Educational Association. Mrs. Robert S. Bradley, also of our Executive Board, is Chairman of the Sanitation Department of the Women's Municipal League, and has led in the fight for exterminating the typhoid fly. Were I to continue to enumerate the characteristic activities of our anti-suffrage women, I could fill pages with the record of their participation in philanthropy, education, and all good works. The brief notes prefixed to the essays in this book give additional evidence to the same effect.

ESSAY I

SUFFRAGE FALLACIES

MRS. A. J. GEORGE

Alice N. George, widow of Dr. Andrew J. George; graduated from Wellesley in 1887; is President of the Brookline Branch of the Ramabai Association; American Representative of the National Trust (English) for the Preservation of Historic Places; a director of the College Club; a member of the Research Committee of the Educational and Industrial Union, of the Welfare Department of the National Civic Federation of the Woman's Trade Union League, of the American Society for Labor Legislation, etc., etc.

J. A. H.

Woman suffrage must ultimately fail. It is based upon a fallacy, and no fallacy has ever made a permanent conquest over mankind.

The fallacy of woman suffrage lies in the belief that there is in our social order a definite sex division of interests, and that the security of woman's interests depends upon her possession of the elective franchise.

"The history of mankind," declared the founders of the suffrage movement, "is a history of repeated injuries and usurpations on the part of man toward woman, having as the indirect object the establishment of an absolute tyranny over her." "Man has endeavored in every way he could," continues this arraignment of the fathers, husbands, and sons of these self-styled *Mothers of the Revolution*, "to destroy her confidence in her own powers, to lessen her self-respect and to make her willing to lead a dependent and abject life."

On this false foundation was built the votes-for-women temple. How shall it endure? The sexes do not stand in the position of master and slave, of tyrant and victim. In a healthy state of society there is no rivalry between men and women; they were created different, and in the economy of life have different duties, but their interests are the common interests of humanity. Women are not a class, they are a sex; and the women of every social group are represented in a well-ordered government, automatically and inevitably, by the men of that group. It would be a fatal day for the race when women could obtain their rights only by a victory wrested at the polls from reluctant men. These truths are elementary and self-evident, yet all are negatived by the votes-for-women movement.

That the vote is not an inalienable right is affirmed by Supreme Court decisions, the practice of nations, and the dictates of common sense. No state can enfranchise all its citizens, and since the stability of government rests ultimately upon a relentless enforcement of law, the maintenance of a sound fiscal policy, and such adjustment of the delicate interweaving of international relations as makes for peace and prosperity, it is right that the state should place the responsibility of government upon those who are best equipped to perform its manifold duties.

Woman's citizenship is as real as man's, and no reflection upon her abilities is involved in the assertion that woman is not fitted for government either by nature or by contact in daily experience with affairs akin to government. She is weak along the lines where the lawmaker must be strong. In all departments where the law is to be applied and enforced, woman's nature forbids her entrance. The casting of a ballot is the last step in a long process of political organization; it is the signing of a contract to undertake vast responsibilities, since it is the following of the ballot to its conclusion which makes the body politic sound. Otherwise political power without political responsibility threatens disaster to all.

Thus far we have made a few crude experiments in double suffrage, but nowhere has *equal* suffrage been tried. Equal suffrage implies a fair field with favor to none—a field where woman, stripped of legal and civil advantages, must take her place as man's rival in the struggle for existence; for, in the long run, woman cannot have equal rights and retain special privileges. If the average woman is to be a voter, she must accept jury service and aid in the protection of life and property. When the mob threatens, she must not shield herself behind her equal in government. She must relinquish her rights and exemptions under the law and in civil life, if she is to take her place as a responsible elector and compete with man as the provider and governor of the race. Such equality would be a brutal and retrogressive view of woman's rights. It is impossible, and here we have the unanswerable answer to woman suffrage theories.

No question of superiority or equality is involved in the opposition to votes for women. The test of woman's worth is her ability to solve the problems and do the work she must face as a woman if the race is not to deteriorate and civilization perish. The woman's suffrage movement is an imitation-of-man movement, and as such merits the condemnation of every normal man and woman.

Doubtless we can live through a good deal of confusion, but it is not on any lines of functional unfitness that life is to be fulfilled. Woman must choose with discrimination those channels of activity wherein "what she most highly values may be won." Are these values in the department of government or in the equally essential departments of education, society, and religion?

The attempt to interpret woman's service to the state in terms of political activity is a false appraisal of the contribution she has always made to the general welfare. All this agitation for the ballot diverts attention from the only source from which permanent relief can come, and fastens it upon the ballot box. It is by physical, intellectual, and moral education that our citizenship is gradually improved, and here woman's opportunities are supreme. If women are not efficient in their own dominion, then in the name of common sense let them be trained for efficiency in that dominion and not diffuse their energies by dragging them through the devious paths of political activity.

Equal suffrage is clearly impossible; double suffrage, tried under most favorable conditions in sparsely settled western states has made no original contribution to the problem of sound government. On the other side of the ledger we find that the enfranchisement of women has increased taxes, added greatly to the menace of an indifferent electorate, and enlarged the bulk of unenforced and unenforceable laws.

Why does double suffrage, with its train of proved evils and its false appraisal of woman's contribution to the general welfare, come knocking at our doors? Not a natural right; a failure wherever tried; demanded by a small minority in defiance of all principles of true democracy; what excuse is there for it?

The confusion of social and personal rights with political, the substitution of emotionalism for investigation and knowledge, the mania for uplift by legislation, have widely advertised the suffrage propaganda. The reforms for which the founders of the suffrage movement declared women needed the vote have all been accomplished by the votes of men. The vote has been withheld through the indifference and opposition of women, for this is the only woman's movement which has been met by the organized opposition of women.

Suffragists still demand the vote. Why? Perhaps the answer is found in the cry of the younger suffragists: "We ask the vote as a means to an end—that end being a complete social revolution!" When we realize that this social revolution involves the economic, social, and sexual independence of women, we know that Gladstone had the prophet's vision when he called woman suffrage a "revolutionary" doctrine.

Woman suffrage is the political phase of feminism; the whole sweep of the relation of the sexes must be revised if the woman's vote is to mean anything more than two people doing what one does now. Merely to duplicate the present vote is unsound economy. To re-enforce those who clamor for individual rights is to strike at the family as the self-governing unit upon which the state is built.

This is not a question of what some women want or do not want—it is solely a question of how the average woman shall best contribute her part to the general welfare. Anti-suffragists contend that the average woman can serve best by remaining a non-partisan and working for the common good outside the realms of political strife. To prove this contention they point to what women have done without the ballot and what they have failed to do with it.

Anti-suffragists are optimists. They are concerned at the attempt of an organized, aggressive, well financed minority to force its will upon the majority of women through a false interpretation of representative democracy; but they know that a movement so false in its conception, so false in its economy, so false in its reflections upon men and its estimate of women, so utterly unnecessary and unnatural, cannot achieve a permanent success.

ESSAY II

THE BALLOT AND THE WOMAN IN INDUSTRY

MRS. HENRY PRESTON WHITE

Sara C. White, wife of Henry Preston White; educated in the Emma Willard School of Troy, New York; a member of the Auxiliary Board of Directors of the Brookline Day Nursery; member of the Committee on Ventilation of Public Conveyances (Woman's Municipal League); With Miss Mabel Stedman of Brookline, Mrs. White started the model moving-picture show in connection with the Brookline Friendly Society. She is a well-known speaker for the anti-suffrage cause.

J. A. H.

The argument that the woman in industry needs the ballot in order to obtain fair wages and fair working conditions has undoubtedly made many converts to the cause of woman suffrage. The sympathies of the average man, who is ever solicitous for the welfare of women, go out especially to the woman who must compete with men in the work-a-day world. And so, when he is told that there are 8,000,000 such women in this country, and that their lot would be much easier if they could vote, he is apt to think it worth a trial anyway and to give his support, without further consideration, to the "votes for women" movement.

Now, if it were true that there are 8,000,000 women in industry, and that these must have the ballot in order to get fair treatment, it would be a strong argument for woman suffrage—though by no means a conclusive argument, since the fundamental question is the greatest good of the greatest number, and not the greatest good of any class. But it is not true that there are 8,000,000 women in industry, and a single sensible reason has yet to be advanced for the contention that women in industry, even if they numbered 8,000,000, could better their condition by undertaking political methods.

There are in the United States, according to the last census, 8,075,772 females 10 years of age and over engaged in gainful occupations. Of these, over 3,600,000 are employed in domestic and personal service, where wage and working conditions are determined chiefly by women, and in "agricultural pursuits," a classification including every female who sells eggs or butter on the home farm. Approximately 4,000,000 of the remaining gainfully occupied females work in store, factory, and shop, and of these nearly 1,500,000 are under twenty-one.

Thus, instead of 8,000,000 women in industry who are alleged to "need the ballot," we have only about 2,500,000 women of voting age employed in industries that can reasonably be said to come within the category of those properly subject to remedial labor legislation; and of these women a very large percentage are aliens and would not be entitled to use the ballot if woman suffrage were granted. By itself, of course, this fact does not dispose of the argument that the industrial woman needs the ballot, but it does reveal how comparatively few are the women who could possibly try to improve their working conditions by means of the vote, and how hopelessly outnumbered they would be if reduced to the necessity of fighting for their rights at the ballot box.

The premise of the suffrage argument that the woman in industry needs the ballot in order to get fair treatment is the assumption that she now fails to get as fair treatment as is given the industrial man, and that this is due to the fact that she has no vote. This arbitrary assumption is without justification either in fact or reason. Every law placed upon the statute-books of any state for the benefit of the working man is a blanket law and covers men and women engaged in the same industry. All the benefits that have accrued to the working man through legislation are enjoyed equally by his sister in industry. In addition she has the advantage of special protective laws which have been enacted simply because she is a woman—because she is weaker physically than man and because she is a potential mother and must be protected in the interest of the race.

I am not arguing, of course, that the working woman has all the protection she needs, but I am arguing that she is not unfairly treated as compared with her industrial brother, who has the ballot, and that whatever hardships she may now suffer are as likely to be removed without woman suffrage as they are with it. If she is being unfairly treated, I think it will be found that she is so treated in common with all industrial workers—simply because she is a worker and not at all because she is a woman.

And in taking this ground I am by no means forced to depend upon theory; for, after all, the best answer to the dogma that the woman in industry needs the ballot in order to obtain fair wages and fair working conditions is the fact that in states where women have voted anywhere from 4 to 46 years the laws for the working woman are no better than they are in male suffrage states. Indeed, it is pretty generally agreed that the states which have been first and most progressive in enacting laws for the benefit of women and children in industry are states that have refused to give women the vote.

It is quite true, as the suffragists so constantly tell us, that the only states having eight-hour laws for women in industry are woman suffrage states. But it is true, too, that the eight-hour laws of California, Oregon, and Washington, of which so much is heard, are not to be taken at their face value, since they do not cover the canning industry, which is the chief industry in all those states. It is true, also, that what is considered by experts the most advanced step in protective legislation for women in industry, the prohibition of night work, has been taken only in male suffrage states. In Massachusetts and Nebraska the laws provide for a 54-hour week for women in industry, provide for one day's rest in seven, and prohibit night work. Will any one deny that these laws are infinitely better for women in industry than the boasted eight-hour law of Colorado, under which it is permissible for a woman to work nights and Sundays and 56 hours a week?

Now as to the question of "fair wages." The suffragists tell us that women in industry are entitled to equal pay with men, and that this will follow upon the heels of woman suffrage. Here again we have experience to guide us, and we find upon investigation that in no state has the ratio between men's and women's wages been affected by doubling the electorate. Dr. Helen Sumner, who made a thorough investigation of this point, says in her book entitled *Equal Suffrage:* "Taking the public employment as a whole, women in Colorado receive considerably less remuneration than men. It is the old story of supply and demand in the commercial world, and suffrage has probably nothing to do with the wages of either men or women. The wages of men and women in all fields of industry are governed by economic conditions."

By tables carefully compiled, Dr. Sumner shows that in Colorado, women in private employment receive an average of only 47 per cent of the average of men's wages, while in the United States as a whole the average for women is 55.3 per cent of the average for men, and in Massachusetts, where woman suffrage was recently defeated by nearly two to one in the largest vote in the state's history, women receive 62 cents for every 100 cents paid to men in wages.

No one can deny, of course, that the wages of women in industry average considerably lower than those of men. But the reasons for this are found entirely outside of politics. The average girl is a transient in industry, going into it as a temporary expedient to tide her over until she attains her natural desire, which is to marry, settle down, and raise a family. She is, therefore, not so good an investment for her employer as the boy who works beside her, who has gone into the business with the idea of making it his life work, and who has a stronger incentive to make himself more valuable.

It must be remembered that employers of labor do not pay for men and women, but for results. Samuel Gompers, an ardent suffragist, says women get less because they ask for less. That is true in part. Women do ask for less. One reason for this is that they look upon the job as something temporary. Another reason is, very frequently, that they are not entirely dependent on their own earnings, but are partly supported in their parents' home. But in the majority of cases, the industrial woman gets less than the industrial man because she is worth less, being not only less experienced, but physically unable to compete with him on a basis of absolute equality.

If the proof of the pudding is in the eating, the proof of woman suffrage is in its operation; and, when we find that it has failed to fulfill its promises where longest tried, it is hard to listen patiently to pleas for its further extension. The vote has never raised the wages or shortened the hours of men. It has never done it and can never do it for women. The industrial woman can gain nothing by it. She will lose much, as will other women.

ESSAY III

A BUSINESS WOMAN'S VIEW OF SUFFRAGE

EDITH MELVIN

Miss Edith Melvin, educated in the public and private schools of Concord and by her father, James Melvin, who, by reason of service in the Civil War was a totally helpless invalid confined to his bed for many years before his death, when he left a widow and an only child dependent upon themselves for support. After three months as assistant to the advertising manager of a large medicine producing company, she entered the law office of Judge Prescott Keyes without business training other than in stenography and typewriting. In this law office has had more than twenty years practical business and legal experience, a position of ever increasing responsibilities requiring steady and efficient study and thought. Not a member of the Bar, never having applied for admission because not believing in women becoming lawyers. Has served as President of the Guild of the First Parish (Concord) and Secretary of the South Middlesex Federation of Young People's Religious Unions. Is an experienced public speaker. Has been an officer and active member of Old Concord Chapter, D. A. R. For many years a householder and taxpayer.

J. A. H.

After more than two decades spent in active business life, I am of the opinion that members of my sex do not need the ballot, and that it would be a distinct and unnecessary encumbrance to them. For more than twenty years, I regret to state, my life has been more that of a man than of a woman. A home-supporter by the actual work of my hands and my brain, rather than a home-maker; my life has been past amid the heat and turmoil of business life, working shoulder to shoulder with men, pitting my brain against the brains of men; and having no male relative to represent me in the business of the government, a taxpayer "without representation." That business life has been satisfactory to me in many ways, I admit; but in order to wrest its satisfactions from the turmoil, I have been forced to summon up the determination, the endurance, the physical and mental labor, which by all the laws of nature belong not to the "female of the species" but to the male. Its successes have been apparent successes when considered as parallel with man's work in the world, but failures when one considers that not for the sharp, insistent contact of business life was woman created. I still feel no desire to assist the male sex in the business of government, nor do I think I am fitted so to do. I desire to be permitted to continue my present freedom from political activities, and I am content to leave that part of life's work in the hands of the sex which, to my mind, has managed it hitherto exceedingly well.

I have never seen any point or place where the power to cast a ballot would have been of the slightest help to me. For myself I should regard the duties and responsibilities of thorough, well-informed, and faithful participation year after year in political matters as a very great misfortune; even more of a misfortune than the certainty of being mixed up in the bitter strife, the falsifications, and publicity often attendant upon political campaigns. Though my work has trained me to use my mind in matters pertaining to law and to business, it would certainly be incumbent upon me to make a thorough study of the theory and practice of government before attempting to exercise the franchise. I feel sure that the average business woman cannot make such a study or engage in politics without interference not merely with her physical, but with her mental business life, which should command her constant and best attention.

Many women are now undertaking to engage in business, not as a life-work, but as an incidental experience. It is true, however, that of the many thousands of women so engaged, very, very few climb up the ladder of success to the top rounds. It is the rare exception rather than the rule for women to attain marked distinction, great wealth, or fame in the business world. This is not caused by any unfairness of the male sex, but by the nature, the physical and mental limitations, of the members of the female sex. The trivialities of the afternoon tea are too often present in the work of the wage-earning woman—too often she has too slight a regard of her duty to return full value for the pecuniary consideration she receives. The career of too many wage earning women is now entirely haphazard, the result of necessity rather than well-grounded choice. It is fair to assume that political matters would receive the same degree of smattering knowledge and thought as is too often received by the daily occupation into which many women drift.

It is much to be deplored that the trend of some modern young women is more towards the commercial life in which her success is doubtful, rather than toward the home-keeping, child-bearing, social, religious, and philanthropic life for which she was physically and mentally designed. These latter duties women faithfully and successfully perform as their natural function, and through them they may rise to the greatest distinction. Femininity should be cherished by the woman whom circumstance or necessity drives into the wage-earning world, and she can cherish it by retaining her hold on social, religious, and charitable interests; but she cannot hope to do so if she attends political meetings, serves on political committees, canvasses districts for votes, watches at the polls, serves on juries, and debates political questions or records and promises of political candidates. We have seen the loss of femininity produced by the constant campaigning for suffrage.

The instability of the female mind is beyond the comprehension of the majority of men. The charm, the "sweet unreasonableness," the lack of power of consecutive thought upon any intricate problem, which mark the average woman are sometimes attractive and in personal or family relations not without compensating advantages. In the business world, however, these attributes are wholly detrimental. Business women might possibly bring to political matters such training and experience as they acquired, but to restrict the franchise to them would be to create a class franchise. We must remember that suffrage would bring to the electorate not merely the small number of business women, but the great mass of women who have had little or no experience of life outside of their homes.

In brief, then, the voting privilege granted to women, and particularly to business women, would be a detriment to the women, and it would not be of sufficient value to the government to outweigh the loss to them.

ESSAY IV

SOME PRACTICAL ASPECTS OF THE QUESTION

ELLEN MUDGE BURRILL

Miss Ellen Mudge Burrill, educated in the Lynn public schools, graduated from the Lynn Classical High School; now in the employ of the Commonwealth as Cashier in the Sergeant-at-Arms Department; Supervisor in the First Universalist Sunday School of Lynn; a member of the Council of the Lynn Historical Society; author of the "State House Guide Book," "Essex Trust Company of Lynn" (the successor of the Lynn Mechanics Bank,) "The Burrill Family of Lynn During the Colonial and Provincial Periods," and of "Our Church and the People Who Made Her," being a history of The First Universalist Parish, Lynn.

J. A. H.

If suffrage were a natural right, then women should have it, and at once, but it is not like the right to have person and property protected, which every man, woman and child already possesses. It is not a natural right, but a means of government, and therefore a matter of expediency. The question is, will government by the votes of men and women together produce better results than by men alone? Suffrage means more than casting a ballot; if it means anything effectual, it means entering the field of politics. Had the proposed amendment been ratified, it would have become the duty of all women to vote systematically in all primary and regular elections. Would they have done it in justifiable numbers?

Look at Public Document No. 43, giving the number of assessed polls and registered voters for the Massachusetts State election of 1914:

Assessed Polls	Registered Voters	Persons Voting
1,019,063	610,667	466,360
Also for the City and Town elections of 1914:		
Assessed Polls, Male	Registered Voters, Male	Males Who Voted
1,229,641	740,871	532,241

It is evident from these figures that a larger proportion of men should fulfill their duty to the State. Government being one means to the end, of making better conditions, the indifference of so many thousand is beyond comprehension, and is a serious menace to the Commonwealth. It was Governor Curtis Guild who said: "I base my anti-suffrage position on the fact that our great failures in legislation are caused not so much by a vicious element among the voters, as by abstention from voting and emotional voting."

That granting the ballot to women would greatly increase the proportion of those who neglect to vote, is clearly shown by the results of giving women the school vote. In 1879 the Massachusetts Legislature, assuming that women were peculiarly interested in school affairs, bestowed the school franchise upon them. See how they have accepted that charge! According to the United States Census of 1910, there were 1,074,485 women of voting age in this State. Of this number there are approximately 622,000 eligible to register and vote for School Committee. Here is the School vote for 1914:

Women Who Registered Women Who Voted
101,439   45,820

Here is the school vote of the women for the city election in Lynn, 1914:

Approximate number of women of voting age in Lynn   18,000
Total registration   1,759
Number of women who voted   1,070

In a pamphlet entitled, "Women and the School Vote," Miss Alice Stone Blackwell, trying to explain away the real meaning of the situation, says:

"A woman's name, once placed on the register, is now kept there until she dies, moves or marries. When a town or city shows a large registration of women and a small vote, it means that on some occasion, perhaps ten years ago, there was an exciting contest at the school election, and many women registered and voted. When the contest was over, many of the women ceased to vote, but their names stayed on the register."

Her conclusion is that this is "the simple explanation of the lessened proportion of women's votes to registration." But a more striking conclusion must be drawn, namely, that it isn't enough to vote when there is an exciting contest; that it is only well as far as it goes, but it should be kept up. The State has a right to expect it. In view of their actual record in the use of the school vote, I see no reason to think that women would vote in sufficient numbers and with sufficient regularity to improve politics or government.

The effect of woman suffrage upon the tax rate must also be considered. If the good to be gained were to justify the expense, there would be nothing to say; but if not, then we ought to pause to give certain facts some thought. Take the expenses for the primary and state elections. The total cost to the Commonwealth in 1914, merely for the preparation, printing, and shipping of ballots, was $50,046.17 (Auditor's Report, 1914, page 240). I am informed that if women were given the ballot, a conservative estimate would add 50% to this figure. If women become candidates for public office, there would be the further expense of handling the nomination papers. And these calculable expenses are only a fraction of the total economic loss.

The City of Lynn has the second largest voting list in the state, outside of Boston. The expense now, for the state and city election machinery and assistants, is $9,000 a year, in round numbers. The amendment would entail nearly double the expenditure. There are 53 cities and 320 towns in the state. Think it over before it is too late. The financial side must enter into the problem some time; isn't the present a good time?

The milk question was referred to several times in the recent campaign, the suffragists implying that the Commonwealth was ignoring the need of legislation and inspection. Here are some of the milk laws on our statute books, that are administered by the State Department of Health:

The Revised Laws, Chapter 56, provide:

Penalties for the sale of adulterated, diseased, or skimmed milk.

Penalties for sale of milk not of good standard.

For the marking of skimmed milk.

For the marking of condensed milk.

Penalty for using counterfeit seal or tampering with sample.

Penalty for connivance or obstruction.

For the sending of results of analysis to dealer.

That inspectors must act on information and evidence.

The following acts are also in force:

To prohibit the misuse of vessels used in the sale of milk (Acts 1906, chapter 116).

To establish a standard for cream (Acts 1907, chapter 217).

To establish the standard of milk (Acts 1908, chapter 643).

To provide for the proper marking of heated milk (Acts 1908, chapter 570).

Relative to licensing dealers in milk (Acts 1909, chapter 443).

To provide for the appointment of inspectors and collectors of milk by Boards of Health (Acts 1909, chapter 405).

Relative to the liability of producers of milk (Acts 1910, chapter 641).

To provide for the inspection and regulation of places where neat cattle, their ruminants or swine are kept (Acts 1911, chapter 381).

To authorize the incorporation of medical milk commissions (Acts 1911, chapter 506).

Relative to the establishing of milk distributing stations in cities and certain towns (Acts 1911, chapter 278).

Relative to the labelling of evaporated, concentrated, or condensed milk (Acts 1911, chapter 610).

To regulate the use of utensils for testing the composition or value of milk and cream (Acts 1912, chapter 218).

To safeguard the public health against unclean milk containers and appliances used in the treatment and mixing of milk (Acts 1913, chapter 761). Relative to the production and sale of milk (Acts 1914, chapter 744).

To prohibit charges for the inspection of live stock, dairies, or farm buildings (Acts 1915, chapter 109).

The State is divided into eight health districts, with an inspector for each in the State employ. Each city has its board of health; each town administers the laws through its selectmen. The City of Lynn has a board of health; also health inspectors, who do much of their work before we are up—from 2 to 5 o'clock. They inspect all the milk stations; take samples from milk wagons; inspect dairies that sell milk in Lynn, wherever those dairies may be, even out of the State—as, for instance, the Turner Centre Creamery in Maine. All that doesn't look as if the milk situation was being neglected.

Massachusetts is doing a great deal for the children. There are over 5,800 wards in the care of the State Minor Wards Department. I do not need to tell you what a great work is being done for the care and education of these little ones; it speaks for itself.

Our opponents do not say much about the work women are doing on State Boards. There are plenty of positions already held by women who are doing inconspicuous and unexciting work, yet, nevertheless, most useful to the Commonwealth. Here are some of them, with the number of women on each board:

The State Board of Health, Lunacy and Charity was organized in 1879, with 2 women on the board.

The work is now divided among different departments.

The State Board of Education had 1 woman member as far back as 1880; it now has 2.

The State Board of Charity has 2.

The Free Public Library Commission has 2.

The Commission for the Blind has 2.

The Homestead Commission has 1.

The Minimum Wage Commission has 1.

The Board of Registration of Nurses has 3.

The Prison Commission has 2, who also serve on the Board of Parole for the Reformatory for Women.

The Board of Trustees of the State Infirmary and State Farm has 2.

The Board of Trustees of the Hospitals for Consumptives has 1.

The State Hospitals at Worcester, Taunton, Northampton, Danvers, Westboro, Medfield, Monson, Boston, Foxboro, have 2 each.

The Gardner State Colony has 2.

The Wrentham State School has 2.

The Massachusetts Training School Trustees has 2.

The Massachusetts General Hospital has 1.

The Perkins Institution for the Blind has 1.

The Hospital Cottages for Children has 1.

Here are forty-five women doing voluntary work on these Boards, all appointed by the Governor and working under laws passed by the *men* in the Legislature.

Take another line. The manual of the labor laws enforced by the State Board of Labor and Industries, covers the enforcement of the laws relative to the education of minors, employment of minors, hours of labor, apprenticeship, hours of labor for women, health inspection, lighting, ventilation, cleanliness, guarding against dangerous machinery, work in tenement houses, etc.

The little book entitled "Woman Suffrage, History, Arguments, Results," tells all about the suffrage states and gives the good laws that have been enacted since women voted. It gives the impression that none such are passed in male suffrage States. It has just two words about Massachusetts; under the heading of "School Suffrage," it says, "Massachusetts—1879." Under California, however, it gives a list of the following laws and institutions:

> Mothers' Pensions.
> Minimum Wage.
> Juvenile Court.
> State Training School for Girls.
> Teachers' Pension.
> Weights and Measures.
> Civil Service.
> State Housing Commission.
> Milk Inspection.
> Tuberculosis.
> Workingmen's Compensation.
> Psychopathic Parole.

But it carefully omits to mention that Massachusetts has all of these, that some of them are much broader in scope, and that many are of longer years standing.

You go into the Western States, and you find that legislation is conducted on a different basis from what it is in Massachusetts. Altogether too frequently, bills are pigeon-holed; the bills can't be reported out of committee unless the chairman consents; and the result is that many bills never see the light. Here in Massachusetts law-making is better managed. The number of bills presented is large; 3,459 were printed during the session of 1914, and 2,802 were printed during the last session. Some of these were offered by women. A woman, as well as a man, can petition the Legislature. Every bill is referred to a committee; it is given a public hearing, is reported upon and action taken, one way or another; not one bill is pigeon-holed. The Massachusetts system of legislative procedure is not surpassed anywhere in the United States, and there are competent boards and officers who carry out the various laws. Many of the things the suffragists agitate about and think they need the franchise to bring to pass, they would find are already being administered at the present time if they would only look into the facts.

ESSAY V

HOW MASSACHUSETTS FOSTERS PUBLIC WELFARE

MONICA FOLEY

Miss Monica Foley, was educated in the Boston schools, graduating from the Boston Academy of Notre Dame; is a member of the Massachusetts Bar and Secretary of the Massachusetts Association of Women Lawyers. She is a director of the Notre Dame Alumni Association of Boston, and is connected with the State Commission on Economy and Efficiency.

J. A. H.

In the suffrage campaign just closed so much was heard of the greatness of some of our states, including Utah and Nevada, Colorado and Wyoming, that one was tempted to inquire, "Is there no good now in Massachusetts?" It seemed passing strange that our Commonwealth, which had always been the leader in every great turning point of the policy of the nation, should have so signally failed that it ceased to exist as a model to be extolled; it was stranger still that her worthy record was ignored by her own sons and daughters. And yet the facts are that while we may hold high in memory the examples of those who have gone before us, we may also rejoice that the men of our own time not only uphold the best ideals and lofty purposes of our State, but are day by day working out her problems in such a way that her position is still secure as a pioneer in sane legislation, her laws are still models for all states (particularly woman suffrage states) her name is still cherished in the wildernesses where her sons are pioneers, still venerated on her own soil where her people stand at the gateways and welcome the oppressed.

Proud as we are of her traditions, glorying as we do in her present achievements, we are unafraid that the future will see her fall from her eminence, from the dignity which has always characterized her statehood and made her name a synonym for the best in government in the nation, our Commonwealth of Massachusetts.

While this paper deals almost wholly with the executive functions of the state, to make no mention of our judiciary would be to omit reference to one of the brightest pages of our history. Massachusetts law and Massachusetts judiciary decisions have always been and are now quoted and respected in the greatest courts of the country. This splendid system is being maintained at an annual cost exceeding $600,000.

Hand in hand with the establishment of a great judiciary system, Massachusetts has devoted herself to the highest ideals of human charity, and her enormous expenditures show that selfish materialism plays no part in her legislation. Year by year the calls for charity are more insistent, and year by year the State responds more generously. The State Board of Charity was first organized in 1863, and at the present time is an unpaid board of nine members, two of whom are women. The institutions under their supervision are governed by unpaid boards of seven members, two of whom are women, this latter being provided by law, except in the instance noted below. The institutions under the supervision of the board are the State Infirmary for the sick poor at Tewksbury, and the State Farm at Bridgewater for misdemeanants and insane criminals, both opened in 1854 and costing the state nearly $1,000,000 annually. The training schools for delinquent children are the Lyman School for Boys at Westborough (1848) and the Industrial School for Boys at Shirley (1909) and for Girls at Lancaster (1856) costing over $300,000 annually. The hospitals for consumptives are located at Rutland (1898), North Reading (1909), Lakeville and Westfield, both the latter being opened in 1910. Upon these suffering poor the State spends over a half million dollars each year. The Norfolk State Hospital at Walpole was opened in 1911 for inebriates and drug habitues. There are no women on this board of trustees, there being no women inmates of the hospital. There has also been located at Canton since 1907 a Hospital School for crippled children. A hospital for lepers has been maintained at Penikese Island since 1905.

Under the direction of the Board of Charity, aid is given mothers with dependent children, the support of poor babies is undertaken, and the tuition of poor children is paid. The board places the children in homes wherever possible—institutional life being approved only when necessary. Certain suffragists (of the Socialist persuasion) would give the children to the State under the new order. In 1914 the Board together with the institutions under their direction expended over three million dollars and cared for more than 7000 persons in the institutions alone. Is there anything here in the State's charity work which would make any woman other than proud of its record?

The State's care of her insane is under the direction of a paid board of three members, each hospital having a board of seven unpaid trustees, including two women. The hospitals for the insane are at Worcester (1833), Boston (Dorchester, 1839), Taunton (1854), Northampton (1858), Danvers (1878), Westborough (1886), Foxboro (1893) and Medford (1896), Gardner (1902.) There is a hospital for epileptics at Monson with schools for the feeble-minded at Waltham (1848), with a colony at Templeton since 1900 and a school at Wrentham (1907). In 1914 the State cared for over 14,000 of these unfortunates and expended over three and one-quarter millions of dollars for their maintenance.

The reformatory and correctional work of the Commonwealth (other than exercised over the training schools) is under the direction of a board of five prison commissioners (two women), only the chairman being paid. Four institutions comprise this group; the State Prison at Charlestown since 1805, but first established in 1785; the Reformatory at Concord (1884); the Women's Reformatory at Sherborn (1877); and the Prison Camp and Hospital at West Rutland, the camp being opened in 1904, the hospital in 1907. Massachusetts has the distinction of being the first state in the union to separate its women offenders from the men, by establishing the Sherborn Reformatory. No child is born at this institution. A mere man a few years ago, realizing the needless handicap an innocent child would suffer through life if born in a prison, petitioned the legislature to prevent the possibility. A law accordingly was passed, and these unfortunate women are placed in a state hospital until after their children are born. In 1914 over 1500 persons were cared for in our prisons at a cost of more than a half million dollars. Two boards of parole now study the histories of prisoners and recommend certain persons for parole, the men's board in addition recommends persons to be pardoned to the governor and council.

In no other sphere of the State's activities is the great throbbing heart of the Commonwealth shown with such poignant fervor as in the case of her unfortunates, and this phase of her work alone would entitle her to the homage of all our people—but she does not stop here. She dominates the educational field, and stands preeminent before the nation and the world for the superiority of her educational institutions.

Massachusetts has given abundantly to the great university at Cambridge, still endows freely the Massachusetts Institute of Technology, and gives annually of her funds to the Worcester Polytechnic Institute, the Textile Schools at New Bedford, Lowell, and Fall River, and other independent industrial schools. She practically maintains the Agricultural College at Amherst, and gives to other agricultural schools, and also aids certain cities and small towns.

In aiding the deaf, dumb, and blind in 1914, Massachusetts spent over $200,000. In 1891 she opened a nautical school to train her young men in seamanship, navigation, and marine engineering. In 1839 Massachusetts founded the first Normal school in this country, and today ten of these schools are open throughout the State. In this line of endeavor in 1914 the State expended over one and one-half millions of dollars.

The Commonwealth maintains a Department of Health, established in 1869, expending in 1914 over $350,000. In Massachusetts also was passed the first pure food law in the country.

The Metropolitan Water Works have cost the State since 1901 over $50,000,000. Our park system is one of the finest in the world, and is maintained at an annual cost of over half a million dollars. In addition to the parks in the Metropolitan District, there are six other reservations throughout the State. These parks represent an outlay of over $20,000,000.

Our Homestead Commission was established to investigate defective housing conditions and study building and tenement house laws. Its members are unpaid, though the labor representative is reimbursed for any loss he may suffer from absence from his regular occupation.

It can truly be said that no State in the union shows such grateful and worthy appreciation to its veterans as does Massachusetts. In 1914 over $700,000 was given to the veterans of our Civil War and to certain of their dependent relatives, and to women army nurses. Under a special gratuities act of 1912 she gave each living veteran of the war the sum of $125, this one act alone costing over $500,000.

Among other of her good works, she appropriates each year $15,000 for the relief of injured firemen and families of firemen killed in the performance of their duty, and since the fund was established has expended $270,000 for this work. The State also provides under a contributory system for its employes.

Nowhere in the country are the people's savings and insurance more zealously guarded than by Massachusetts, and here again she is leading the way in the savings bank life insurance legislation. The bank commission was established in 1838, the insurance commission in 1855, the savings bank life insurance board in 1907, these three departments costing in 1914 almost $200,000.

In dealing with her labor problems Massachusetts maintains a Department of Labor and Industries (1913) which investigates industrial conditions and enforces the labor laws; an Industrial Accident Board (1912) which enforces law compensating injured employes. These two boards together constitute a joint board for the prevention of industrial accidents and diseases. There is also a Board of Conciliation and Arbitration (1886) which mediates and arbitrates industrial disputes, and a Minimum Wage Commission (the first in the country), which investigates the wages of women and minors, and forms boards to recommend scales of wages in low paid industries. Over $200,000 was expended by these boards in 1914.

On encouraging farming and caring for her forests, fisheries, and game, was spent over $600,000 in 1914. This was distributed in many ways, some being in form of bounties to children and youths, to agricultural societies to encourage orcharding, poultry raising, for the purchase of forest lands, the prevention of forest fires, the propagation of wild birds and animals.

Preparedness was not overlooked, over half a million dollars being expended on the militia in 1914. On highways and harbors nearly a million dollars was spent.

Over a million and a quarter dollars was spent on public buildings, the total valuation of state properties being over $8,300,000, the State capitol and land itself being valued at over five and one-half million dollars.

This is the record of Massachusetts. The suffragists have shown wisdom in avoiding reference to these facts. They could not well do otherwise, however, since they are allied with those detestable groups in our midst who are preaching anarchy and revolution as a means to better government. Better government where? This record is one that the men of the State may well be proud of; it is a record that its women will continue to make possible by their non-partisan influence in government, by the training of its future citizens, by the teaching of those lessons of civic honesty and uprightness that make for national integrity as exemplified in the history of our Commonwealth of Massachusetts.

ESSAY VI

MASSACHUSETTS COMPARED WITH SUFFRAGE STATES

CATHERINE ROBINSON

Miss Catherine Robinson was a student at Radcliffe in 1911; graduated from Miss Wheelock's Kindergarten Training School in 1915; has worked two winters among the children in the cotton mills of Georgia, and has been affiliated with Neighborhood House in East Boston, and with the Associated Charities in the Co-operative Workrooms. She is now connected with the Social Service Department of the Massachusetts General Hospital, her work being in the Orthopaedic Clinic for Children. Miss Robinson was formerly a suffragist, but after studying the question decided that the suffragists' claims are illusions which never become realities. She says: "Everything I do along these lines (Social Service) convinces me more than ever what a detriment the vote would be to our sex."

J. A. H.

Not long ago I heard Dr. Anna Howard Shaw, the President of the National Woman Suffrage Association, say at Springfield:

"Laws have nothing to do with this question of woman suffrage; facts have nothing to do with it. I shall not answer facts. We do not promise to do great things for women; why should we? All we ask is the right to vote."

All suffrage speakers are not so frank about their inability to answer facts as Dr. Shaw is, nor do they cease from claiming that good laws for women exist chiefly in suffrage states.

Massachusetts gives to her women the best protection of any state in the Union. In January, 1915, New York ranked first, but since our legislative enactments of 1915, Massachusetts is again in the lead. We have, in the first place, the Maternity Act. Then we have the law prohibiting women in industry from working more than fifty-four hours per week. We have the absolute prohibition of night-work for our women in textile, mercantile, and manufacturing establishments. We are one of the five states in the Union to have such a law. All the five states are male suffrage states. Not a single woman suffrage state prohibits the night employment of its women; and yet among the laws safeguarding the health of women workers, the prohibition of night work is of the most fundamental importance.

Some women suffrage states do not even set a limit to the hours a woman may work. In Wyoming, Nevada, and Kansas—all woman suffrage states, you note—there is no limitation of hours of labor and no prohibition of night work. Some one may say that Colorado, California, Oregon and Washington have an eight-hour limitation. They have; but in each case the canneries are excepted, so that in those states where the cannery business is of vast importance, the women therein employed may work any number of hours and any time of the day or night. Not long ago in New York a similar law was proposed, allowing women and children to work seventy-two hours a week in canneries, but the bill was defeated. Colorado, to be sure, has the eight-hour law, but it does not prohibit night work for women, so that the eight hours can be at night; neither does Colorado require one day of rest in every seven. In Massachusetts and New York there is a law specifically requiring one day of rest in every seven for employees in factories, workshops, and all mercantile establishments.

Another way in which we can protect women is by early closing hours, and prohibition of work before a certain hour in the morning. Again we find that it is in the male suffrage states that women have acquired such protection, for New York sets an early closing hour of 5 p. m. for her women in factories, mercantile, and manufacturing establishments, and Massachusetts sets 6 p. m. Fourteen other male suffrage states set 10 p. m. as the closing hour; and all these states prohibit work before 6 a. m. What do we find in the woman suffrage states? Simply that out of the eleven suffrage states, one state, California, sets a 10 p. m. limit, but it does not apply to canneries.

As women enter further into the industrial field, more and more laws are made for their protection. The men have done wonderfully for our women. Whenever the public conscience is aroused to the need of a law, that law is passed. Women do much, in fact, nearly everything, towards arousing that public conscience, but we find when we study the laws as they exist in our state that our men have made better laws for the protection of our women than the men and women have made together in any suffrage state. Let me add some of the other good laws we have in Massachusetts. We have the Mothers' Pension Bill. This law was originated by a man in a male suffrage state. We have the Equal Guardianship Law. There are suffrage states where neither of these laws exist.

Not long ago Mrs. Maud Wood Park, asserted that I was misstating the laws in suffrage states. She said I did not know the happenings in the legislature this year. I have made a careful study of the laws proposed and the action taken upon them in the eleven suffrage states and the four big "campaign states" in the legislative year of 1915. I find that while in Massachusetts we enacted *five* new laws relating to our women and children assuring them of still greater protection and better public health regulations, Arizona turned down five laws for women which already exist here in our own state. I was unable to find any suffrage state which could compare in any favorable way with the progress Massachusetts has made. Wyoming turned down a bill regulating the employment of children and a bill limiting the hours a woman may work. As long as I have mentioned Arizona, let me continue the comparison one step further and point out that on the 16th of February, 1915,

Mrs. Berry, an Arizona suffragist, introduced a bill regulating and granting teachers' pensions. The bill was indefinitely postponed. In the same year Massachusetts women teachers introduced a bill asking to have their former pensions granted again to them. At the same time the men teachers introduced a similar bill; and it is an interesting fact that the men were turned down, while the women's bill was signed by the Governor. For our suffrage friends who say that women must have the ballot to be listened to, this is rather a stumbling block. I happened to be up at the State House the day the bill went through, and heard one of the women who was interested say: "It's a mighty lucky thing we women did *not* have the vote." This is the latest example of what Massachusetts men are interested in doing for Massachusetts women. Let us voice our just pride that Massachusetts touches the high water mark of protective legislation and stands as an example to all other states.

ESSAY VII

WOMAN SUFFRAGE AND WAR

MRS. CHARLES P. STRONG

Mary B. Strong, widow of Dr. Charles P. Strong of the Harvard Medical School; studied for three years at the Massachusetts Institute of Technology; former President of the Saturday Morning Club; Vice-President of the Cambridge Indian Association; Corresponding Secretary of the Massachusetts Women's Anti-Suffrage Association.

J. A. H.

When the great European war broke out in 1914, the suffragists tried to use the situation to further their propaganda. They remind me of the mad philosopher who suggested it would be well to profit by an eruption of Vesuvius in order to boil an egg.

The incongruity of suffragists attempting to pose as a peace party is obvious to anyone with a memory and a sense of humor. Before the war broke out, American suffrage leaders were applauding, feasting, and subsidizing the British virago who instigated the setting on fire of 146 public buildings, churches, and houses, the explosion of 43 bombs, the destruction of property valued at nearly two million dollars (not including priceless works of arts), and many cases of personal assault. In 1912 they justified the destruction of the Rokeby Venus; in 1914 they professed horror at the bombardment of the Cathedral of Rheims. Is this insincerity or hypocrisy, or mere aberration of mind?

The best time to work for peace is before war breaks out. The suffrage organization was not conspicuous in seizing the many opportunities for furthering the cause of peace before it was too late. In 1911 Mrs. Frederick Nathan, a prominent suffragist, was asked to contribute to the American Society for the Judicial Settlement of Disputes. She sent the following characteristic refusal:

"Mrs. Frederick Nathan prefers to give her money to the Woman Suffrage Association.... She has no faith in Courts of Law and Equity which deny justice to women."

Was this boycotting of the peace movement condemned by the suffragists? Not at all; Miss Alice Stone Blackwell, President of the Massachusetts Suffrage Association, was glad to print the refusal in the official organ of the National Woman Suffrage Association. Miss Blackwell, in holding up this example to its members, scornfully declared that several of the peace society were "prominent opponents of equal rights for women." In those days, the suffragists were not hitching their wagon to the quiet star of peace; it has been their constant practice to attach themselves, for publicity's sake, to whatever movement is conspicuous on the front pages of the newspapers—eugenics, or sex drama, or red-light abatement, or what not—and to abandon that ephemeral interest whenever it has ceased to serve the purpose of advertisement.

And so, when the war broke out, the boycotters of peace societies, and colleagues of militants, made a rapid shift of costumes, and tried to play roles in the Woman's Peace Party. So hurried was their change of mental attitude that their thoughts on the subject were splendid instances of snap judgment.

In truth, the breaking out of the war was most embarassing to them. Like a bull in a china shop, the rush of brutal fact destroyed many of their pretty theories. The stereotyped suffrage answer, when anti-suffragists pointed out that physical force was the fundamental basis of government, had been that this was no longer true. For example, Dr. Mary Putnam Jacobs, speaking of women's demand for the ballot, said, about 1895: "Women could not claim the ballot while it was necessary to defend opinions by arms, but this is no longer necessary or expected." And Mrs. Susan Fitzgerald in 1912 declared: "The age of the fighting man is passing. The world is coming to be ruled by intellect." When will the suffragists learn Lowell's maxim: "Don't never prophesy—onless ye know!" It is, however, a characteristic of professional false prophets not to lose their imperturbality and effrontery, but to trust that their followers will forget their mistaken guesses and listen open-mouthed to a new dispensation.

The essential dogma of the Woman's Peace Party (none but suffragists admitted!) was that the adoption of woman suffrage was a necessary and effectual step toward abolishing war. "If women had had the vote in all countries now at war," said Mrs. Catt, "the conflict would have been prevented." History shows women at least as much inclined to war as men—a fact illustrated in the French Revolution, in our Civil War, in the Franco-Prussian War of 1870-71, and in other instances too numerous to mention. The suffragists, ignorant of that fact, or ignoring it, advanced in support of their proposition a series of specious arguments designed to catch popular opinion. Of these arguments two were at the outset of the movement especially harped upon: (1) the alleged "international solidarity of women," and (2) the supposed likelihood of woman's opposition to militarism.

What was meant by the "solidarity of women" is explained in Mrs. Pethick Lawrence's words: "The interests of women, being fundamentally the same, are so universal that no national distinctions can cut deeply into them, as may possibly sometimes happen with the national distinctions between men." Following that notion, Dr. Anna Howard Shaw issued an appeal to the women's organizations in the belligerent countries, urging them to put a stop to the war. The replies received showed that the expected "international solidarity of women" was imaginary. The Association of Austrian Women's Clubs, for example, replied that nobody understanding the causes of the war, would have addressed such a request to them. "Being women of those countries," ran this reply, "where our husbands, brothers, and sons are fighting for the existence or non-existence of our state, for our homes, for their wives and children, we cannot say: 'Do not fight'!" Similarly, the women's societies of France refused to accept any invitations to peace palavers. In short, the real "solidarity" was discovered to exist, not between women of different nations, but between the women and the men of each nation.

The falsity of the other argument—that woman suffrage would tend against militarism—was crushingly refuted when Dr. Ernest Bernbaum drew attention to the recent history of militaristic policies in England and Australia. In male suffrage England, Lord Roberts, despite his personal popularity and strong arguments, was unable to get sufficient support for his program of universal military service. In woman suffrage Australia and New Zealand, on the other hand, the same line of arguments was completely successful by 1911. There, boys from their twelfth year are required to be enrolled for instruction in drill and the rudiments of military science. The penalties for failure are severe, and public opinion supports their enforcement; in New Zealand a boy was sent to jail for refusing service, on ground of conscientious scruples; another was fined and went into exile. The electorate was determined that New Zealand and Australia should be nations in arms; indeed they were more drastic than Germany, where many exemptions from military service on various grounds are allowed. It is instructive to recall that when in March, 1914, Winston Churchill, Lord of the Admiralty, advised Australia that, in view of the Japanese alliance, it did not need to spend as much money on warships, the Australian statesmen frankly intimating their distrust in alliances, declared they would proceed with their expensive naval program, which was supported by both political parties. I do not say that what is termed "militarism" is a bad policy; I do say that when the suffragists state that woman suffrage tends against militarism they state what is diametrically opposed to the real truth of history. In this case, as usual, they draw their principles not from observation of what is happening but from what they wish and fancy would happen.

The theories of the Suffrage Woman's Peace Party being false, it is not surprising that their actions prove bewilderingly futile. They brought together a group of "hand-picked" delegates, quite unrepresentative of the real sentiment of the nations they were nominally representing, and forgathered in a so-called Woman's Peace Conference at the Hague. Miss Jane Addams supplied the American press with rose-colored accounts of its proceedings. Her reports were justly condemned by the New York Times as bad journalism, because they did not "tell the whole of the truth." They were calculated to give the impression that the Conference was harmonious, and that its deliberations led to really practicable conclusions. Not to conceal the truth, it must be said, that these pacific ladies, who surely ought in their own circle to have exhibited that "international solidarity" which the sex as a whole had failed to manifest, soon developed sharp antipathies. One of the few British delegates who went to the conference (need it be said she was not Mrs. Pankhurst?) disturbed its complacency by reminding those present that they really did not represent the sentiments of the warring nations. When it came to discussing the actual situation and specific terms of peace, there arose strong differences of opinion—along national lines. The chief resolution offered,—that peace should be made without delay,—could not be passed until an amendment, adding the words "with justice," was accepted,—words which each belligerent would interpret in a different manner. Needless to say, the amendment rendered the high-sounding resolution a useless mass of ambiguous words.

Equally futile were the subsequent travels of the delegates of the Woman's Peace Party. At a time when the energy and money of every woman should have been whole-heartedly devoted to practical deeds of charity, these misguided women wasted their means and strength in fool's journeys to the capitals of all the great nations. They made proposals for immediate peace negotiations, which were listened to with more patience and politeness than their amateurish character deserved, but which were of course without exception pigeon-holed.

Having moved the nations to mirth by one modern version of "Innocents Abroad," the suffragists appear to have thought it a good advertisement to send forth a second. This time they attempted to screen themselves behind the figure of Mr. Henry Ford, wearing a celluloid button, "Out of the Trenches by Christmas!" But when a man acts with apparently inexplicable foolishness, it is generally safe to say, "*Cherchez la femme!*" In this case, the truth presently came out: the unfortunate Mr. Ford was merely the "angel" of the new travelling troupe. It was Mme. Schimmer, professional suffragist-pacificist, who had persuaded him to launch his argosy. As Mr. Ford himself confessed on his ignominious return, he was "simply backing up and financing the plans of the Woman's Peace Congress." The second expedition, like the first, developed an astounding fighting spirit among the peace delegates, and accomplished nothing. (It is worth noting that woman-suffrage Denmark prohibited the party from holding any public meetings.)

There is a lamentable as well as ridiculous aspect of the suffragists' activity in connection with the peace movement. Their intrusion into the pacificist camp has brought discredit not only upon themselves, but upon every pacificist. If the word "pacificist" today suggests to most men an ecstatic, irresponsible dreamer, it is they who are to blame. The sane pacificist, whose patient labors are directed toward unsensational and unspectacular, slow but sure, organization of friendly relations to be gradually made closer and closer, realizes that his task is a complicated one, not to be solved by emotionalism, but by calm reasoning and patient adjustment. He realizes that many different functions must be brought into co-operation before the likelihood of war can be reduced. His noble work is in danger of being thought ridiculous because of the meddling of suffrage fanatics.

The present war, instead of justifying the suffragist theory, has refuted it. It has vindicated the position of the anti-suffragists.

What is the chief lesson of the great war? It has shown that international law and treaties are so weak as to be useless, unless there is physical force to ensure their not being violated. What anti-suffragists have always maintained in national government has proved true in international relations. Any law that is made by those unable to support it through force of arms will sooner or later become a "scrap of paper." Consequently the most sanely progressive step in the peace movement is the formation by men like Mr. Taft, and Mr. A. Lawrence Lowell, (both anti-suffragists, by the way) of a league to enforce peace, which aims to give international law the sanction not only of world-wide opinion, but of the irresistible power of the united armed forces of the great nations. That is the work of men toward world peace.

What is the work of women? In this field as in all others, it is not to try to compel, but to educate and civilize, to create in the children committed to her care an intelligent love for fair play, justice, and self-control. The suffragist is an enemy to the diffusion of the peace spirit, because she would force women into political warfare, where contention is bred. She closes her eyes to woman's greatest opportunity for diminishing the spirit of belligerency—that of keeping one of the sexes out of the bitter strife of partisan politics. The anti-suffragist, asking that the mothers of men may be left free to develop the milder attributes of character, has the true vision of the road that leads to lasting peace.

ESSAY VIII

WOMAN SUFFRAGE VS. WOMANLINESS

MRS. THOMAS ALLEN

Alice Ranney Allen, wife of Thomas Allen; member of the Woman's Municipal League, in which she was the organizer of the Department of Streets and Alleys; member of the Woman's Education Association; reader of the Committee on Selection of Fiction for Libraries; Chairman of Boston Committee on the work of District Nursing in the mountains of North Carolina; a well-known speaker against woman suffrage.

J. A. H.

To me the chief reason why political duties should not be imposed on women is the effect that this preliminary dip into politics, this struggle for votes-for-women, is having on the women themselves. It is surely not making them any more lovely, or pleasant in their lives. They grow bitter, aggressive, and antagonistic, liking the excitement of campaigning and finding their natural, proper duties "flat, stale, and unprofitable."

Speaking from platforms and being constantly in the public eye, does not improve women. We anti-suffragists have taken part in a political campaign to keep ourselves out of politics for the rest of our lives, and to keep our daughters out of politics, but we know that in a proper division of duty we have better work to do along civic, sanitary, and philanthropic lines, and in our homes, than to be, as our Western sisters are, out campaigning for candidates, and engaged in struggles for political supremacy.

Anyone may gauge the bitterness of the recent campaign if he remembers the abuse heaped on the anti-suffragists by the President of the National Suffrage Association; and we must judge every movement by its leaders. Dr. Anna Howard Shaw, at a hearing before the Senate Committee at Washington, said:

"We are not afraid of the body of women who are going up and down the land opposing suffrage. They are just enough in number so that by holding out their skirts they can make a screen for the men operating dens of vice and iniquity and prostitution to hide behind."

In an interview printed in the New York Sun, Dr. Shaw referred to the anti-suffrage leaders as "vultures looking for carrion."

As important a person as Dean Thomas, of Bryn Mawr College, in an appeal for funds for the National American Woman Suffrage Association in February, 1913, said:

"The ballot for women is the greatest of all the modern reforms. We urge those who are today contributing to other causes to *withdraw* or *curtail* their contributions until the ballot for woman is secured." This seems to us anti-suffragists extremely narrow, as we know that woman suffrage is not a reform, but an experiment in legislation only.

In a public resolution passed by the New England Women's Suffrage Association at its forty-seventh annual meeting, the anti-suffragists were referred to as using "pole-cat" tactics—why, we do not know. These are only a few of the many evidences of the bitterness of feeling in this political campaign.

The whole ideal of womanhood seems to be changing. The wife of an editor of our most important New England magazine said to me:

"What use is it for you to oppose the suffrage movement, when it is only the first step in this larger movement for the emancipation of women that is sweeping over the world?" And I said: "Then we will do our best to stop the first step," for I remembered the doctrines of the suffrage leaders preached from their platforms. Mrs. Ida Husted Harper has said: "There is not a single forward step of woman that has not been blocked by the words 'wifehood' and 'motherhood'."

Dean Thomas, in an address to women at Mount Holyoke College, is quoted in Mr. Martin's book, *The Unrest of Women,* as saying: "Women may have spent half a lifetime in fitting themselves for a scholar's work, and then may be asked to choose between it and marriage. No one can estimate the number of women who remain unmarried in revolt before such a horrible alternative."

Dr. Stanton Coit is reported as saying from a suffrage platform: "Wifehood has all the characteristics of slavery—work without wage; no specified hours; no right to change employers."

We find constantly the evil influence that this first step of suffrage is having on the young women of our day; and, to me, the gist of the whole matter seems summed up in a paragraph from a pamphlet written by Mr. Joseph Pyle:

"With Christianity there came into the world a new example and a new thought. To woman's whole nature appealed that life of self-sacrifice, of love, and of willing service that has created a new Heaven and a new earth. From the foot of the Cross there arose and went out into the world a womanhood that did not demand, or claim, or threaten, or arrogate; a womanhood renouncing, yielding, loving, and, therefore, conquering. For twenty centuries that has been the law of woman's life. It is sneered at and rejected today by the clamorous, but it has made of woman what we now find her. You see it in your mothers, your daughters, your wives. Do you wish to have that ideal changed? Woman has become to man not only a companion, but an inspiration. Out of the crucible of the centuries has come what we not only love but adore; before which, in certain hours, we bow with a reverence that links us unconsciously with the Divine. It is Christian civilization that is in the balance."

ESSAY IX

ARE SUFFRAGISTS SINCERE REFORMERS?

MRS. AUGUSTINE H. PARKER

Caroline M. Parker, wife of Augustin H. Parker; was educated in the Boston schools; is a member of the Dover Grange; Vice-President of the Unitarian Alliance of Dover; for five years President of the Vincent Club.

J. A. H.

If the energy and vast sums of money squandered to promote suffrage in this country had been expended to bring about the reforms which the suffragists claim will be at once brought about by their votes, the reforms would all have been accomplished long ago. But do the suffragist leaders care a jot about the reforms? We hear of a Seattle woman who, now that she can vote in her own city, leaves home and husband to come East and agitate for suffrage. Little does she care that her husband sues for divorce on the ground of desertion. It is the excitement of agitation that she craves—the duties and responsibilities of the ballot are of no interest whatsoever to her.

A mayor in a city near Boston appointed a suffragist on the city planning board. Did she eagerly grasp the chance to plan the city so that it should be a joy and a blessing to its inhabitants for all time? Not at all. She said that the mayor did not consult her, that she had not even known there was a city planning board, and that she would not think of serving on it in any case.

Through the Civic Federation, the Municipal Leagues, and the Women's Clubs, an enormous amount of work for the good of all has been undertaken; but the suffrage members of these associations far from welcoming all public spirited workers, attempt to make the belief in woman suffrage the test of a worker's value, and introduce party politics and petty strife into these great, non-partisan bodies of women, thereby impairing their services to the Commonwealth to such an extent that the eyes of many women have been opened to what the state of affairs would be if all women were in politics. It is not too much to say that many women, hitherto indifferent on the suffrage question, have been aroused by such interested and partisan methods into joining the anti-suffrage cause.

There is more work waiting to be done than there are workers to do it. Ministers are constantly asking from the pulpit for workers. There are more offices open to women now than there are women to fill them, but they are the offices that mean hard work and no notoriety, and these are not what most of the feminist-suffrage leaders are looking for. These feminists tell you constantly how badly the men manage the country; the idea being how much better the women would govern it. But would they? The anti-suffragists think that, on the whole, the men are doing well, and that a government ought to be in the hands of those who have the power to enforce the laws they make. To have responsibility without power is to be in a very uncomfortable and ignominious position. To the observer it seems that the professional suffrage agitator is *not* out for service or the good of her town, state, and country, but for her own good. This is so obvious that her self-assertion is not convincing. It is through service and not by self-assertion that true women contribute their best work to their country.

Because they are unconvinced by the feminist's protestations, few women care to be represented by other women. Approximately half the stock of the Pennsylvania Railroad is owned by women. They could elect several women directors if they wished to do so, but the board is composed entirely of men. Women do not as a rule, employ other women to take care of their business affairs.

We anti-suffragists ask to be left free from the useless turmoil of partisan politics so that we may employ what time and strength we have in the service of those who need them most. We do not care to waste them in the petty personal struggles of the political arena—we can well afford to let the men fight the battles and crowd the polling booths because we in our own places and to the full extent of our power, have an equally valuable contribution to make to the welfare of the nation.

The help of all good women is now at the service of the men who have the nations' welfare at heart, nor are they hampered by the interference of the less good as they must be when the vote of the best might be nullified by the vote of the worst.

We beg the men not to be deceived by the noise and clatter of a few paid professional agitators, supported by misguided enthusiasts whose hearts are larger than their heads; and we ask the men to help us to uphold the womanhood of woman with all its responsibilities, its ideals, and its spiritual endowment.

ESSAY X

SUFFRAGE AND THE SCHOOL TEACHER

ELIZABETH JACKSON

Elizabeth Jackson graduated from the Bridgewater High School in 1908, from the Bridgewater State Normal School in 1910, from Radcliffe College A. B. (Summa cum laude) 1913, A. M. 1914; is a candidate for the degree of Ph. D.; treasurer of Radcliffe Chapter of Phi Beta Kappa 1914-16; President of the Radcliffe Graduates' Club, 1915-16.

J. A. H.

An essential weakness in the suffrage argument is the failure to distinguish between government and culture, the functions and the instruments of each. Government is an organization for compelling one portion of the community to do the will of another portion. In a democracy, the minority is forced to obey the majority. The fundamental idea is compulsion, a thing not lovely in theory and frequently unlovely in practice. The golden haze that surrounds the dream of ideal democracy is dissipated by contact with any given city ward. The machinery of government is a matter of stress and strain; of selfishness, cruelty, and hate, at the worst; at best, of conflicting interest, mutual incomprehension, and maddening friction. When we refer to good government, we may mean either of two things. We may perhaps describe a community where the majority is notably successful in imposing its will on the minority so that laws are strictly enforced and scrupulously obeyed. In my experience, this is not the sense in which the suffragist uses the phrase. Woman suffrage is not advertised as a means of producing a more tractable minority. On the contrary, as Mr. Taft has pointed out, the suffrage movement is a conspicuous instance of one great menace of the age, the unwillingness of minorities to abide by the best judgment of the state as a whole. Again, the campaign orator does not assure the Maine audience that under equal suffrage statewide prohibition, instituted by male voters, will become a fact instead of a joke; no speaker in our home town has informed us that woman's vote will wipe out the saloons that defy the "no" of the March meeting. Rather, as I understand it, the "good government" which the suffragist promises to inaugurate consists of improved legislation along certain specific lines. That is to say, she promises not that the laws will be better enforced, but that they will be different. A community's predilection for good laws or bad, however, depends not on government but on civilization. Public opinion is moulded by innumerable forces, of which the home, the church, the newspaper, and the public school are merely illustrations. In most if not all of these, women already play a conspicuous part; through them they wield an incalculable power. The confusion, unconscious or otherwise, of these forces of culture and the forces of government, is one of the prime fallacies of the suffrage position.

To make the true state of the case more clear, take a single institution, the public school, with its various bearings on the question of woman suffrage. Pass over the school committee vote which only about two per cent of Massachusetts women regularly use, and consider merely the power which the very nature of our school system puts in women's hands. All the children in our primary grades, and all but an infinitesimal fraction of those in the grammar grades, are taught by women. The preponderance of woman teachers is nearly as great in the high schools where, except in a few cities, men are employed for administration and discipline and only secondarily for instruction. That is to say, women and not men are shaping the minds of future voters during the formative and decisive years. From women rather than men, our children learn the elements of good citizenship, — respect for public property, obedience to law, and the power of independent thought.

The degree to which the lesson is learned, depends upon two things; namely, the quality of the teacher and the extent of her influence. Accordingly, two questions arise. Would woman suffrage give us better teachers? Would it increase the power which they already hold? One may get some light on the first point by studying the placing of normal school graduats. The connection between the schools and politics is already lamentably close. Many districts, with administrations predominantly of one party or religious sect choose first teachers of that sect, good or bad, and sisters and daughters of voters of that party; then enough women to complete the necessary number. Suppose that the teacher, instead of being the daughter of the voter, holds the vote herself. The evil would become universal. There is no indication that a woman's salary and position under such circumstances be more directly conditioned upon her abilities as a teacher. The chances are that woman suffrage would tend to make the school more truly the servant of the party in power than of the general good. Moreover, a vote can be used as a commodity of exchange; and the woman-voter who amid the fluctuations of city politics would protect her position by a shrewd use of her ballot would hardly be the best school mistress of American youth.

The effect of suffrage upon the teacher's influence in the schoolroom would not be beneficial. Her treatment of some subjects, like grammar, nature study, and raffia work, would of course remain unchanged. It has, however, been said by suffragists that her discussion of civic problems would be more intelligent. Would her judgments be cooler because she is in the thick of the fight, and her statements more convincing because she is in direct conflict with the fathers and mothers of half her class? It is of the utmost importance that the child shall look upon the teacher as impartial. He may consider her in some respects his natural enemy, but he must none the less regard her as one of the immutable things of the universe. For this reason public commotions over school affairs, however well intentioned, injure the institutions they design to benefit. Anything which tends to increase the possibility of opposition between the teacher and the child's family, and makes the child's attitude partisan is a menace. Suffrage in this field as in so many others, offers no compensation for the increased friction and unrest.

ESSAY XI

SUFFRAGE AND THE SOCIAL WORKER

DOROTHY GODFREY WAYMAN.

Dorothy Godfrey Wayman, wife of C. S. Wayman; was educated at Bryn Mawr and at the School for Social Workers in Boston; has done organized charity and settlement work in Fitchburg and Boston; was for one year state organizer of the Massachusetts Womans' Anti-Suffrage Association; is a member of Massachusetts Civic League.

J. A. H.

Among people who have what has been called "the sheep type of mentality," it is frequently asserted that since Miss Jane Addams, Miss Julia Lathrop, Dr. Katherine Davis, and other "servants of humanity" are suffragists, it follows that all women should become suffragists. Such people do not, however, carry this line of thought to its logical conclusion; for even they do not consider themselves bound to become Progressives because that is Miss Addams's political party, nor to become members of her church.

This *argumentum ad hominem* has great weight in the suffrage propaganda, and it is high time that it should be considered less superficially. Having been a social worker myself in a large city, I have been much interested in the history and career of such workers, and find therein one of the most positive anti-suffrage arguments.

It is a striking fact that the very women whom suffragists use as personal exhibits accomplished the social work that won them fame, under male suffrage. Conversely, in the long list of women's names honored for their social service, not one of national reputation earned that reputation in a woman suffrage state.

The National Institute of Social Science awards a gold medal for distinction in social service. Men like William H. Taft and Charles W. Eliot have been thus decorated. Miss Jane Addams, Miss Lillian D. Wald of the Henry Street Nurses' Settlement in New York, Miss Mabel Boardman of the National Red Cross, and Miss Anne Morgan of New York are the women who have been presented with this medal in past years.

On February 25, 1915, the National Institute of Social Sciences conferred this medal for distinction in social service upon Miss Louisa Schuyler of New York City. In a long life of useful citizenship, though unblessed by the ballot, Miss Schuyler has contrived to inaugurate several undertakings and lived to see them grow, till from radical innovations, they have become the groundwork of much of our modern charity. Miss Schuyler discovered the shocking conditions prevailing in almshouses fifty years ago, and organized a series of volunteer visiting committees which eventually became the N. Y. State Charities' Aid Association, with headquarters in New York City. Miss Schuyler was the organizing genius of the Bellevue Visiting Committee, which from visiting the poorhouses of Westchester County, progressed to the establishment of the first training school for nurses in this country. Trained nurses have come to be such a necessity today, that I imagine few suffragists realize that they are indebted to one woman's initiative for the ministrations of skilled hands that so often may mean the difference between life and death. Today there are 1100 training schools for nurses, whose existence can be traced to the ideas of a woman living and working in a male suffrage state. Another feat, more political in its aspects, accomplished by Miss Schuyler was the inauguration of the system now in force of State care for the insane, and of the removal of insane persons and children from the physically and morally degrading atmosphere of the almshouse where they were formerly cared for. In 1908, Miss Schuyler grappled with another of our great modern problems and organized the first committee in this country, composed of physicians and laymen, for the prevention of blindness. What a long way behind the world would be today if Miss Schuyler had done as Dr. Anna Howard Shaw, and devoted her great organizing genius to suffrage propaganda!

Miss Jane Addams' achievements in Chicago at Hull House, are too widely known to require any enumeration, but I would emphasize the fact that her work was done while Illinois was still a male suffrage state. In *Twenty Years at Hull House*, which was published in 1910, three years before women attained partial enfranchisement in Illinois, Miss Addams gives her estimate of the field of a settlement in social work for a community: "It seems impossible to set any bounds to the moral capabilities which might unfold under ideal civic and educational conditions. But, in order to obtain these conditions, the Settlement recognizes the need of cooperation, both with the radical and the conservative, and from the very nature of the case, the Settlement cannot limit its friends to any one political party or economic school." Since these words were written, Miss Addams has allied herself definitely with a political party, at great loss of personal prestige, but that does not alter the truth of her written opinion. The end of every public spirited woman is identical with that of the Settlement, "to obtain ideal civic and educational conditions" for her community; and "the very nature of the case," as Miss Addams says, demands that they be not obliged to limit their friends to any one political party, but remain free from political affiliations in order that their disinterestedness may not be cavilled at.

Miss Lillian D. Wald's work as a district nurse at the Henry Street tenement she chose to occupy on graduating from her training course as a nurse showed the way to the efficient Visiting Nurses' Associations that are being organized today all over the country, and also to the public recognition of the value of instruction in health which is finding expression in the staffs of nurses maintained in many cities by the Board of Health and School Departments whose services are free to the people. This humanitarian work manifestly had no connection with the ballot.

Miss Kate Barnard, the "Girl Commissioner of Charities" in Oklahoma, is a striking figure of our day. The neighboring state of Kansas is a woman suffrage state, yet Miss Barnard seems to prefer residence in the male suffrage state of Oklahoma and has done great things there. When Oklahoma was admitted to statehood, it was Miss Barnard who wrote the child labor, prison reform, and other humanitarian measures into the State constitution; and she was made State Commissioner of Charities, which position she holds today. Miss Barnard, too, recognizes the power for evil of partisan politics. She is at present waging a bitter fight for the property rights of the Indian wards of her state, and writing in the *Survey*, says: "I want the people of the U.S. to stand by me until the hand of *partisan politics* is wrested from the control of Indian affairs in Oklahoma and in the nation."

In 1912, when the Children's Bureau was established at Washington, we might have expected that one of the women constituents of the petticoated West would be placed at its head. Instead, President Taft appointed Miss Julia C. Lathrop, a resident of Hull House in Chicago, and a former member of the Illinois State Board of Charities, where she was credited with the enlargement of the Illinois State charitable institutions and their thorough reorganization, though, of course, obliged to work without the ballot. Time has proved the wisdom of Mr. Taft's appointment and also borne witness to the peculiar advantage enjoyed by women in politics, provided they are not shackled with the ballot.

One of the thought-inspiring books of 1914 was also a splendid argument for the anti-suffragists. It was *Beauty for Ashes*, Mrs. Albion Fellowes Bacon's account of the securing of the Indiana Model Housing Act, which was accomplished through the initiative and leadership of this one woman, mother, and home-maker, with no political prestige, with no previous reputation built by long publicity, without the all-powerful ballot.

Mrs. Bacon was supported by the Federated Woman's Clubs of her State, and enlisted the aid of earnest men and women citizens throughout the State. Her bill was bitterly contested by the worst class of landlords, but after three sessions of the Legislature, at which Mrs. Bacon was obliged to appear in person and explain her bill, it was passed. She says of that day: "The women, the homes of Indiana, were honored that day by the men of the Legislature, and we had won a law for the 101 cities of our State. No wonder the women applauded as some of the men who gave their reasons, added 'and because the women wanted it'." Her conclusion is: "Most strongly have I desired to show how much can be done by women's organizations by simply demanding right legislation, and to show their equally important part of helping to enforce legislation after they get it."

Speaking of her own work, she says: "Having no hand in the management of political affairs, I may leave to the various political parties the care of reaping the thorns in each other's fields. It has been my pleasand task to gather only the grapes.... I have encountered more figs than thistles, and fewer thistles than what seems to be a sort of cacti, that, I firmly believe, might be Burbankized for human good. Would that they might be, and that we might include in the conservation of vital resources those great powers for good that are now so wasted by constant warring for political supremacy."

That last sentence forms a scathing indictment of the shortsightedness of suffrage policy. It is pitiful to think of the energy and ability which today is diverted from channels of human helpfulness to this sensational struggle for a mistaken cause. It is not to be thought of that we can permit woman's energy to be permanently dissipated in political warfare or handicapped by party vicissitudes.

These examples of achievements by women of our own day, in our own country, should convince the clear thinker that woman's contribution to community organization and progress is best accomplished as a non-partisan. The stories of Miss Schuyler and Mrs. Bacon prove that whenever a woman has a righteous cause or a sane ideal, she will be successful in its realization without the ballot. The three women cited above whose work most depended on legislation for its accomplishment, Miss Addams, Miss Barnard and Mrs. Bacon, have all in their penned words lauded the power of non-partisanship.

And, borrowing from Miss Barnard, the anti-suffragist may say to the woman who seeks to enfranchise her sister, thus destroying the power of that great, womanly contribution towards the solving of the vexed questions of the day made by the disinterested, because disfranchised citizenness: "Stand by me till the hand of partisan politics is wrested from the control of society's charities, till prisons, almshouses, children's homes, public hospitals, are administered for the public good rather than private profit; till decent housing, progressive education, adequate recreation, pure food, living wages have been made a matter of public, rather than political, concern." Let us not dissipate our energies in internecine warfare, nor yet seek to perpetuate the drawbacks of our partisan system of government by enfranchising the women who now stand outside politics.

ESSAY XII

WOMAN SUFFRAGE A MENACE TO SOCIAL RE-FORM

MARGARET C. ROBINSON

Margaret Casson Robinson, wife of Professor Benjamin L. Robinson of Harvard University; President of the Public Interests League of Massachusetts; President of the Jaffrey Village Improvement Society; Vice-President of the Cambridge Hospital League; Vice-President of the Friends of Poland; member of the Executive Board of the Cambridge Anti-Tuberculosis Association; Editor of the "Anti-Suffrage Notes," and a frequent contributor to the press.

J. A. H.

The truth of our anti-suffrage doctrine that woman suffrage will destroy the present non-partisan power of women and give us nothing worth having in its place is constantly confirmed by the current happenings in suffrage states. We have now, in the eastern and middle states, a body of non-political women workers of incomparable value, and one is amazed at the wrong-headedness which would deprive society of their influence. Under present conditions the intelligent woman interested in public affairs brings the full force of her influence to bear upon legislation; her influence is a moral influence—it is direct and can be used with men of all political parties. The possession of this unprejudiced, unrestricted power is something which anti-suffragists value so highly that the threat of the suffragists to destroy it is a very serious grievance.

It is surprising that social workers and club women in larger numbers are not awake to this danger; but, as has well been said, deciding wisely on this question is not a matter of intelligence but of information; and it is easier to accept suffrage theories and the *mis*information which suffrage orators generously supply as to how suffrage *will* work than to study the happenings in suffrage states and learn for oneself how it *does* work.

Social workers and club women know their present strength and how many good laws they have helped to put on the statute books. What they seemingly do not realize is how quickly this power will be gone when they divide into political parties. Many of them are apparently too ignorant of politics to understand that *as voters* it is only those men for whom they will vote that they can influence.

A despatch from Topeka, Kansas, describing the recent campaign in that state says that three years ago the Kansas Federation of Women's Clubs lined up solidly for suffrage, and won it—and that they have not been lined up solidly for anything since! Instead of throwing their influence as a unit for good legislation, as women's clubs are wont to do in male suffrage states, these women are divided into Republicans, Democrats, Progressives, and Socialists, and the friction among them is greater than ever before.

At the time Jane Addams joined the Progressive party it was very striking that such ardent suffragists as Ida Husted Harper and Edward Devine, editor of "The Survey," should have protested publicly in the strongest terms against her action. They realized perfectly that political partisanship narrows a woman's sphere of influence, and that Miss Addams as a member of the Progressive party could exercise much less influence upon Democrats and Republicans. She had before been able to reach men of all parties, but now her field had suddenly become immensely restricted in its scope. And while Mrs. Harper and Mr. Devine were perfectly willing, even eager, that other women should enter politics and ally themselves with political parties, Miss Addams was too valuable to the causes they had at heart, namely, suffrage and social service, for them to view with equanimity such a narrowing of her field of influence.

In an article on the "Legislative Influence of Unenfranchised Women," by Mary R. Beard, which appeared in the "Annals of the American Academy of Political and Social Science," for November, 1914, Mrs. Beard, although an ardent suffragist, admits that women without the vote have been a strong influence toward good legislation. She says:

"National as well as state legislation has been affected by women, if the testimony of men like Harvey W. Wiley is accepted. In his campaign for pure food laws, he stated repeatedly that his strongest support came from women's organizations. That support was not passive and moral, merely expressed to him privately, but these women inundated congress with letters, telegrams, petitions, pleading for the passage of the laws in question. These communications were presented to congress by their recipients who often urged as their reason for supporting pure food laws the appeals of women whose interests in food should not be ignored.

"The Consumers' League of New York helped the national food committee to defeat a mischievous amendment to the Gould bill, which requires that all package goods should be labelled as to the amount of their contents.

"Mrs. Albion Fellowes Bacon, of Indiana, practically single-handed, secured the first tenement house laws of value for Evansville and Indianapolis. She did this before the National Housing Association, of which she is now a director, was formed. The recent improvements in the Indiana housing legislation are due apparently to her continued leadership and to the public opinion which she has helped to create. In her case it was personal initiative and moral persuasion.

"Another example of personal influence on legislation exerted by women is that of Frances Perkins, of New York, in her fight for the fifty-hour bill for the women workers of her state. Unlike Mrs. Bacon, Miss Perkins represented a society—the Consumers' League—which asked for this measure, and she was supported in her demand by the Women's Trade Union League and other organizations. The measure would have been defeated, as is widely known and acknowledged in New York, had it not been for the personal sagacity and watchfulness of Miss Perkins.

"The social service committee of the 'American Club Woman' states that in the first year of its existence it has done important and effective work. It was largely responsible for the passage of an ordinance by city councils regulating dance halls.

"Similar activities, both positive and negative, can be discovered in the records of practically every woman's association not organized for purely literary purposes."

We all know that this is true. Mrs. Beard also says:

"The woman's influence lies not in physical force, but in the occasional subservience of the mind of man to the actual presence of a moral force."

The influence of this moral force is so strong and has come to be so well recognized that certain types of politicians and commercial interests rebel against it. They wish to destroy it, and as the best means to that end they advocate—woman suffrage! That is not at all in line with what one is told at suffrage meetings. We are told that women need the ballot in order that they may improve the conditions in the home, that they may help the working girl, and put through good legislation. But the rank and file of suffragists are being deceived in these matters, for suffrage works, and will work directly the other way. The New York World has committed a great indiscretion and has let this cat out of the bag. The World recently came out for suffrage and gave its reasons. One of them is that a few women, representing perhaps ten per cent of the sex, have under present conditions too much influence. These women, the World says, "have maintained at times a reign of terror over legislative bodies, in consequence of which half the country is now bedeviled by some form or other of harem government, and legislators are forever making ridiculous concessions to women agitators." These "women agitators" are, of course, the club women, social workers, and others interested in social welfare. In order to make it unnecessary for legislators to make "ridiculous concessions" to this type of woman, the World advocates—what? Giving the vote to all women! It has certainly hit upon the most effective expedient, and it is because the vote will do exactly what the World claims for it, that anti-suffragists are so opposed to it. The World says that most of the reasons urged in favor of suffrage are fantastic and unreal, that women are not purer and more noble than men, and that they are not so wise as men in general affairs. It admits that they will not purify politics—indeed, that they will confuse and disorganize government, without reforming it; but nevertheless it believes in woman suffrage because it will destroy the power of the ten per cent of women whose influence is now so strong!

The question for intelligent women to decide is whether or not they *want* this influence destroyed. If they wish to give up the moral influence which a body of women, educated, public-spirited, non-partisan, can wield—an influence so strong that legislators feel obliged to make what the World calls "ridiculous concessions" to it—if in its stead they wish to depend on political influence gained through the ballot, which can be applied only to one party, which can be entirely offset by the votes of women who are ignorant, boss-controlled, and whose votes are purchasable—if they prefer that, they will get their wish if woman suffrage wins. That is exactly how it is working out in the suffrage states. In Wyoming the politicians were clever enough to foresee this. Woman suffrage was granted by one of the most corrupt legislatures Wyoming ever had. These men knew that at that time good women were few in that sparsely settled State, and they knew they could "manage the others."

Nevada is offering us a most perfect example of the good woman's loss of influence by entering politics. The easy divorce laws of that state, in force until three years ago, were a national scandal. This was realized by certain women of the state, who in consequence brought their moral influence to bear upon the legislature for the repeal of these laws. Their efforts were successful and the laws were repealed. Woman suffrage was granted in Nevada last fall, and one of the very first acts of the legislature was to re-enact the easy divorce laws! These women again protested, but with no success. They were now voters, and the legislature knew perfectly well that plenty of women's votes could be secured to offset those of the protesting women. The moral influence of this minority of Nevada women who cared for social betterment was gone since the vote had been given to all women.

In her admirable anti-suffrage address before the Maine legislature at the recent hearing on suffrage, Mrs. J. F. A. Merrill said:

"What do men do when they want to bring about a reform?

"They do as the men of Portland did a short time ago, when a number of citizens became convinced that the moral conditions in Portland were not what they should be. And what did they do? Did they vote about it? Did they form party organizations? No; they resorted as nearly as they could, to what is known as 'women's methods,' and formed a non-partisan citizen's committee, just as detached as possible from politics. And why did they resort to women's methods? Simply because they had all had the vote since coming of age, and they all knew how useless it is as a means of accomplishing reform work.

"Gentlemen, in every community there are a handful of women who can be relied upon to carry on church and philanthropic and reform work; but we all know that the vast majority are indifferent, and that they neither help nor hinder. And then there is a third class, of women—the wrongminded. They do not hinder reform work now, because they cannot.

"But, gentlemen, when you give the ballot to all women your handful of earnest women in each community, who are willing to give their time and thought to reform work, will have only their handful of ballots to cast for reform measures; your great mass of indifferent women will be indifferent still, and will omit to cast their ballots, and your very considerable number of wrongminded women will have had a weapon put into their hands which they will not omit to use against your reform measures, because it is of importance to them to see to it that their way of life is not interfered with.

"So for the sake of reform which women have done in the past, and ought to be able to do in the future, we beg of you not to tie their hands and hamper them by giving suffrage to women!"

That is the matter in a nutshell—and proofs of the correctness of this statement are constantly multiplying. In an attempt to prove that woman suffrage will not lead women to neglect their homes, a writer signing herself "Annie Laurie" says in the San Francisco Examiner:

"I've been in Denver when a good man was being maligned and almost robbed by political enemies, and he needed the vote of every good woman in town to keep the good work he had done from being stultified. And do you think you could get a single woman out to vote for that man if she wanted to go to a 'tea' or to stay at home and knit socks for the new baby? You could not."

This is just what anti-suffragists maintain—that the great body of home-making women will not vote.

The Woman Citizen, a suffrage publication of California, in its July issue, bears testimony on this question as follows:

"There are today many women in California and other States of the union who, being enfranchised, are too indifferent to vote. We are loath to believe that these women—thousands of them in the United States—are aware of the wrong they are doing. We do not think they know they are shirking a fundamental duty of citizenship. Too many ballots are cast in the cause of dishonesty and corruption. Honest and law-abiding citizens must exert their united strength at the polls to uphold honesty and good government. There are too many women today who are priviliged to vote, yet refrain from doing so either because they do not believe a woman should go to the polls, or because for some inexcusable reason they have neglected to register. They regard their franchise as an invitation to a bridge party, something they can accept or reject as their fancy dictates."

There is no lack of testimony that the wrongminded women do vote. On November 4, the day after election, the San Francisco Examiner said: "McDonough Brothers had several automobiles busy all day long hauling Barbary coast dance hall girls and the inmates of houses on Commercial street to the different booths, and always the women were supplied with marked sample ballots."

They were outvoting the women reformers!

What is the result? What is happening to moral conditions in San Francisco since women vote? The American Social Hygiene Association pointed out last spring that there had been an *increase* in the number of questionable dance halls, and the "Survey" of April 10 stated that danger signals were being flashed all over the country to young people bound for the exposition, as there was much unemployment, and the city's moral condition gave cause for anxiety.

A later report, by Bascom Johnson, counsel of the Social Hygiene Association, who was sent to San Francisco for further investigation, appears in full in the September issue of "Social Hygiene." It is far more serious than previous reports. Within the exposition are several concessions, maintained despite protests specifically against them, which are deplorably vicious. In the city itself conditions are appalling, the policemen being there apparently to prevent anything from interfering with the orderly and profitable traffic in vice.

Summing up his report, Mr. Johnston says, *"in spite of announcements of officials to the contrary*, San Francisco remains one of the few large cities of this country where prostitution is frankly and openly tolerated. The natural and inevitable result has been that San Francisco has become the Mecca of the underworld, and that for every such addition to her population the problem is rendered that much more difficult."

These are the conditions in a city where women vote! Mr. Johnson says that the Y. W. C. A., the W. C. T. U. and other organizations of the kind have tried to improve these conditions, but have failed, as they received *"little or no support from the city officials."* This fact is directly in opposition to the suffrage theory that women must have the vote in order that city and state officials shall pay heed to their wishes. If California were still under male suffrage—if the thousands of dissolute women in San Francisco who will vote as the party in power dictates did not have the vote—the moral influence of the ladies of the Y. W. C. A. and the W. C. T. U. would be much more likely to be a factor in the situation. If these ladies vote at all, their vote is divided between the Democrats, Republicans, Progressives, and Socialists, and is therefore of much less importance than the big vote which can be controlled. Dr. Helen Sumner, sent by the suffragists to study conditions in Denver several years ago, states that "the vote of these women to whom the police protection is essential is regarded as one of the perquisites of the party in power."

With these facts in mind it is very clear that the statement constantly made by suffragists that after women are enfranchised they need not vote if they do not want to, is shallow and unprincipled, and the woman who makes it proves herself an unsafe person to be enfranchised. The stay-at-home vote is a great and serious menace.

Voting differs from the higher education and other so-called "woman's rights." They are privileges only. Whether a girl goes to college or does not go to college is a personal matter, and her decision works no danger to other girls or to the community. The college is there, and she can go or not, as her taste and circumstances decide. But voting is a totally different matter. Enfranchisement confers a privilege and an obligation, the obligation being inseparable from the privilege. Since the shirking of this obligation means a serious menace to the community, the unwillingness of a large majority of women to accept the obligation is a factor of the utmost importance in the situation.

The San Francisco Chronicle says: "Results show that in this state women refuse to accept the obligation which at their request, or upon their apparent acquiescence, has been imposed upon them, or to discharge the resulting duties. The question, then, for the people of other states to decide is the light of experience of the western States is whether it is in the public interest to impose on women imperative duties which the great majority of them refuse to discharge after they have been imposed upon them."

Another danger connected with woman suffrage is this—the character of the women chosen for the positions of responsibility will change.

The Woman's Journal of March 20, 1915, speaking of Mayor Harrison, of Chicago, says: "If he had occasion to appoint a welfare worker for women and children, he did not appoint a woman who had experience for the work and could do it well, but picked out a woman who would be a cog in his political machine." Naturally! It is when women are outside politics that they are appointed on their merits. When they have the vote those are naturally chosen who are cogs in the political machine.

The suffragists never tire of quoting Julia Lathrop. As she holds an important position as head of the Federal Children's Bureau, they consider her views on suffrage, since her views coincide with theirs, as most valuable and important. What *is* important is the fact that if Miss Lathrop were allied with a political party she would not be holding the position which is supposed to give her views such weight. It was only because she was a woman and a non-partisan that she retained her position at the change of administration, when the Republicans went out and the Democrats came in. Every *man* at the head of a similar bureau lost his job!

Miss Jane Addams, in a suffrage speech in Boston, claimed that by means of the ballot women in Chicago have accomplished several important reforms. These were:

1. Covered markets had been secured where food might be kept clean.

2. A court for boys of 17 and under 25 had been established.

3. Public wash-houses have been established.

4. The garbage dumps have been abolished.

The record of accomplishments of Chicago women voters as presented by Miss Addams is not impressive, for the reforms she cites have been accomplished in other cities without votes for women.

What the women accomplished in Chicago *before* they got the vote makes a much more impressive showing. It is to them, says the Chicago Tribune, that Chicago owes the kindergarten in the public school, the juvenile court and detention home, the small park and playground movement, the vacation school, the school extension, the establishment of a forestry department of the city government, the city welfare exhibit, the development of the Saturday half-holiday, the establishment of public comfort stations, the work of the Legal Aid Society, and the reformation of the Illinois Industrial School. This is a long and brilliant list of women's achievements, not to be matched by the voting women of any state. Chicago women were working together when these things were accomplished—now they are fighting each other in rival political parties.

Henry M. Hyde, a reporter for the Chicago Tribune, which has long supported the woman suffrage movement, wrote over his own signature his impressions of last spring's election in Chicago, and the part women played in it. He says:

"The first mayoralty campaign in which women voters participated failed to develop the refining and elevating influence which the sex was expected to exert. When one sees a woman of dignified presence and cultivated appearance greeted with torrents of hisses and insults from the frenzied lips of both men and women;

when one sees her finally driven from the platform with no chance of speaking a word, one is tempted to retire to some quiet spot for a moment and meditate on what it all means.

"When one watches a venerable lady trying to quell the tumult by waving a flag and almost dancing to the same rhythm, while 1,200 shrieking men and women order her to 'sit down and chase herself,' one remembers his own grandmother, and makes a feeble effort to blush. One is almost tempted to pick that discarded and discredited old relic once known as masculine chivalry out of the scrap heap, and see how many people would recognize it."

These references are to a woman's political mass meeting, which was described in a Chicago despatch to the Boston Herald as follows:

"A demonstration approaching a riot marked the women's political meeting here today, and was ended only when the managers of the theatre where the meeting was held dropped the steel curtain and a spectator sent in a riot call for the police."

Does this sort of thing tend to increase woman's influence in uplifting and benefiting her community?

A suffrage writer said recently that the son who grows up to find his mother a voter will have a broadened respect for womanhood. With these scenes in Chicago in mind, do you think he will? Suppose she has just voted for Bath-House John, the notorious candidate who got a majority of the women's votes in his ward, or in favor of saloons, as thousands of women have done—will he have added respect for her? This same writer says: "It might be a new and stimulating experience for a man to have to explain to his wife just why he was voting on the side of a corrupt boss, in favor of the liquor traffic, or against the suppression of child labor." But if she had just done those things herself—and in Chicago the women voted just as the men did—why should the experience be a stimulating one?

Jane Addams, while on her foreign mission of "Peace—with suffrage" said in London, on May 12, 1915:

"I am a strong supporter of woman suffrage, and, although I hope to see the women of England enfranchised, I see around me endless opportunities for social work which could be usefully performed while the vote is being won."

The interesting point about this is that English women have for many years had the vote on all matters pertaining to housing, care of the poor, sanitation, education, liquor regulations, police, care of the insane, care of children, etc. Probably Miss Addams does not know this. They have failed completely to do with the vote what even Miss Addams, confirmed and prejudiced suffragist that she is, admits that they could do perfectly well without the vote. This is certainly a striking admission on her part.

Why have they failed so lamentably? Mrs. Pethick Lawrence tells us. She says:

"I never saw so many women working for social betterment as I have seen in the American cities I have visited. *In England women have turned their attention to politics and have accomplished nothing like so much in civic reform.*"

Anti-suffragists ask women not to turn their attention to politics and neglect civic reform; not to make this appalling mistake, which will set back the social progress of our cities for many years; not to make powerless, through woman suffrage, as the New York World wants to do, the women who are now working for social betterment.

The suffragists apparently do not care what evils follow, provided they get their way.

The Rev. Anna Shaw, president of the National Suffrage Association, says:

"I believe in woman suffrage whether all women vote or no women vote; whether all women vote right or all women vote wrong; whether all women will love their husbands after they vote or forsake them; whether they will neglect their children or never have any children."

In introducing this astounding statement, Dr. Shaw declared: "I believe I speak for the thousands of women belonging to the national association."

Perhaps she does. At least no one of them has been heard to deny it; but fortunately she does not speak for the 24,000,000 women of voting age in the United States who are not members of the National Suffrage association. Many of these do care for public welfare, for social well-being, and for human happiness, all of which would be destroyed if all women voted wrong, if they deserted their husbands, and neglected their children. Anti-suffragists protest against having political power put into the hands of women with no higher ideals than those of Dr. Shaw and her followers. They neither wish to be ruled by such women nor do they wish to have to wage an eternal fight not to be ruled by them, and one thing or the other will be necessary if the ballot is forced upon women. In California the men are begging the home-making type of women to come out and fight the political women, whom they already recognize as a danger and a nuisance.

Men who believe in fair play will refuse to force political life upon all the women of their states because a small fraction think they want it. Those who care for the political welfare of their states will decline to adopt this innovation, which assuredly cannot stand the tests of rational criticism and of experience. If they value in the slightest degree the assistance which educated, public-spirited women are able to give in securing enlightened legislation, they will certainly not favor votes for women; for what woman suffrage does is to take the power out of the hands of these women, who without the vote exert a strong moral influence toward good legislation, and put the power gained through an increase in the electorate into the hands of the bosses who can control the largest woman's vote.

"Practical politicians" are learning this lesson rapidly. The New York Commercial calls attention to the fact that in our cities the female vote is more easily manipulated than the male. This fact does not escape the bosses, and they are rapidly coming into line for woman suffrage. While woman suffrage was largely an untried theory suffragists could maintain with some plausibility that woman's vote would be cast for moral and humane legislation, and would purify politics; but with the actual conditions in Chicago, San Francisco, Reno, Denver, and Seattle what they are, this theory no longer holds water, and it is becoming increasingly evident that the way to do away with the moral influence of women in public life is to give the vote to all women.

ESSAY XIII

THE ANTI-SUFFRAGE IDEAL

MRS. HERBERT LYMAN

Ruth Whitney Lyman, wife of Herbert Lyman; studied two years at Bryn Mawr; a member of the Woman's Municipal League of Boston and of the Board of Directors of the North End Diet Kitchen.

J. A. H.

Women today find their sex disquieted by deep unrest. Our sex is seeking to adjust itself to new conditions. Suffrage, feminism, militancy, have been the symptoms of the first phase of modern woman's attempt to adjust herself to twentieth century conditions. That phase was the outgrowth of hasty judgment, and is rapidly giving place to the second phase, wherein the sober second thought of the normal woman is repudiating the false values preached by those women who impulsively leaped to the conclusion that man's sphere was more potent than woman's and therefore more desirable.

The struggle over woman suffrage presents the spectacle of two camps of women arrayed against each other with opposing ideals. Let no one be so simple as to suppose that the issue is one between men and women. It is not a "woman's rights" question; it is a *which* woman's rights question. Two types of women are at war, for although both desire the same end — namely, a better world to live in — they differ fundamentally as to the method of attaining it.

The fundamental difference is this — that the suffragist (like the socialist) persists in regarding the individual as the unit of society, while the anti-suffragist insists that it is the family. Individualism is the all-important thing to the suffragist; to the anti-suffragist it is soundness of family relationships. Suffragism is founded upon a sex-conscious individualism and sex antagonism, which leads it to say that woman can only be represented by herself, and that women now are a great unrepresented class. As a matter of fact, women are not a class, but a sex, pretty evenly distributed throughout all the various classes of society.

Anti-suffrage is founded upon the conception of co-operation between the sexes. Men and women must be regarded as partners, not competitors; and the family, to be preserved as a unit, must be represented by having one political head. The man of the family must be that representative, because government is primarily the guarantee of protection to life and property and rests upon the political strength of the majority, which should be able in times of need to force minorities to obey their will. That is the only basis on which a democracy can endure. Suffragism says that in order to attack existing evils women must organize for participation in law making. It stakes its faith on more government (a second resemblance to socialism), upon control by law. The anti-suffragist sees the evils of society as fundamentally resulting from the evil in individuals, and calls on women to check it at its source. They emphasize the power of individual homes to turn out men and women, who, trained to self-control, will not necessitate control by law. Knowing well that the great training school for private morality is family life, the anti-suffragist seeks to preserve conditions making for sound family life, the sum total of private morality being public morality, the conscience of the people.

Moreover, the twentieth century has given us its watchword, which is, differentiation or division of labor. Anti-suffragists by accepting it, and applying to their sex the new demands of specialization, put themselves abreast of the times; but suffragists lag behind, still harping on the exploded theories of equality and identity. The strikingly progressive message the new century presents us is this: Give equal opportunity to men and women for expression along their *different* lines. Government, law making, law enforcement, with all the allied problems of tariff, taxation, police, railroads, interstate and international relationships, etc., must still be the business of men. The business of women must be to work out a national ideal of domestic life and juvenile training. They must standardize the family life with their new understanding of the importance of the product of every separate family to the state.

The suffragist, who is so often the unmarried or childless woman, here objects that women could also vote. But it is practically impossible for women as a sex to undertake the regular and frequent political duties. If the highest efficiency in private life is to be striven toward, women must regard themselves as a sort of emergency corps, prepared to meet the unexpected; for illness, accidents, temptation, sorrow—all the disturbances of domestic life—do not come at stated intervals. Anyone can readily see that for women private duty would constantly conflict with public duty. To become an efficient political unit, a woman would have to set aside much time and strength upon organizing and bringing out the woman's vote. There would be the splitting up of women into rival political groups on class, race, or religious lines, the dissipation of energies and strain of contention for women who in America already reach with sad frequency the breaking point of nerves and body.

In contrast to such obligatory activity for all women, consider the field of voluntary non-partisan activity now open to the single woman, the woman of leisure, and to every woman at such times as her family duties permit. Indeed the germ of the true woman's movement lies in the activities of such organizations as education societies, playground associations, municipal leagues, and so forth, which are only in their first stages of usefulness. Here is ample scope and outlet for talents and energy.

Our sex, if kept out of politics, has the opportunity in these days when we prate so much about peace, to set about disarming distrust and discord within our own borders. Shall we not dream of a united American womanhood? We twentieth century women may take a noble stride toward it, if we will, by working for those causes that disregard the divisions of race, religion, and politics. Is it surprising that the anti-suffragist sees a vast, unexhausted field for woman's influence outside the political? No wonder that to the suffragist's craving for a new sphere and new rights she opposes the plea of old duties unfulfilled and existing opportunities neglected.

To contrast the opposing ideals of the two groups of women, let me quote from what a great Frenchman said in the time of the French Revolution: "You have written upon the monuments of your city the words Liberty—Fraternity—Equality. Above Liberty write Duty; above Fraternity write Humility; above Equality write Service; above the immemorial creed of your Rights inscribe the divine creed of your Duties." I truly believe that the women who, perceiving present duties imperfectly performed, refuse to take up the cry for more rights, are following the more Christ-like ideal. I do not think that twentieth century American women have outgrown His peerless example, which urges them to be faithful first over a few things as He commanded. God made us women; and if we are told that women suffer more than men in peace and war, let us answer, "Very likely—Christ Himself found His cross heavy—let us bear the cross and crown of womanhood in His name."

ESSAY XIV

THE TRUE FUNCTION OF THE NORMAL WOMAN

MRS. HORACE A. DAVIS

Anna Hallowell Davis, wife of Horace Davis; was educated in Boston private schools and is a graduate of Radcliffe College; was a member of Local School Board No. 46, New York City, for eight years; is a member of Brookline Civic Society, the North Bennett Street Industrial School Association, and of the Massachusetts Peace Association.

J. A. H.

The whole question of suffrage and anti-suffrage is significant chiefly as it affects the married woman with children and a home; for if there is any elemental fact on which to plant our feet, it is that the normal woman is a wife and mother and home-maker. But is not the contention of the suffragists fundamentally based upon the circumstances of the woman who is not leading this normal life,—who is unmarried, who has no children, or who is not making a home and bringing up her children herself? It is in planning for these exceptional women, as I think they do, that the suffragist leaders tend to ignore the truly representative women—the majority. Do we not suspect, indeed, that they are turning to new ideals, because they have never tried the old? As Chesterton says: "The ideal house, the happy family, is now chiefly assailed by those who have never known it, or by those who have failed to fulfil it. Numberless modern women have rebelled against domesticity in theory, because they have never known it in practice."

"But," the suffragists ask, "granting that your woman of 'normal' life is in the majority, and doesn't want the vote, *oughtn't* she to want it? Casting a ballot takes next to no time, and that is all she needs to do. Most men do no more than that."

But men ought to do more. That is just the point. That is just why corrupt government has been fastened on our cities. The Tammany leaders do more. They give all their time to politics; but the "reform" vote cannot, except occasionally, be got to the polls in sufficient numbers; and too few of the best men will run for office. If women are simply going to aggravate these conditions, if the "normal," representative woman isn't going to vote and hold office, and the non-representative, exceptional woman is, where is the advantage to the state of adding women to the electorate? Probably, however, rather than have this happen, the representative woman would feel that she must enter the lists. In competition with "abnormal" or unscrupulous women, she would be forced to vote and to hold office. More than just going to the polls, she would have to think, read, and talk politics, as men do, or ought to do. The whole question here is: Is it better for her to do this, or to do the things which men don't do? *For one person can't do it all well.* A good mother of three or four children already has more than she can do well. If she takes up this whole new department of life and thought, I am convinced she will have to let something else go, and already under the influence of the feminist movement, that "something else" seems to be her home. So, this is what the anti-suffragists feel most keenly—that once the franchise is imposed as a duty, they would have to do the things which men already are doing (and doing as well as the women could do them); that they would no longer be free to do what they think is the higher work for them, as women. Therefore, when a suffragist tells me she has a "right" to vote, I say that, in the name of the best interests of the community, I have the right *not* to vote.

Another thing which the anti-suffragists feel is not recognized sufficiently by their opponents, is the essential and valuable difference between men and women in their manner of approach to any given human problem. "Law" to the antis seems a man's word. Man thinks of people in masses. He makes laws for the whole. He generalizes better than women. On the other hand, where woman is stronger than he is in her feeling for the individual person, and her use of love rather than of law, neither the masculine nor the feminine gift is better, the one than the other, but the two work together as necessary parts of one whole. As Ida Tarbell puts it: "Human society may be likened to two great circles, one revolving within the other. In the inner circle rules the woman. Here she breeds and trains the material for the outer circle, which exists only by and for her. That accident may throw her into this outer circle is, of course, true, but it is not her natural habitat. Nor is she fitted by Nature to live and circulate freely there. What it all amounts to is that the labor of the world is naturally divided between the two different beings that people the world. It is unfair to the woman that she be asked to do the work of the outer circle. The man can do that satisfactorily if she does her part, that is, if she prepares him the material. Certainly, he can never come into the inner circle and do her work."

So, in claiming for women the right to take a part in the man's half of life, the suffragists, I think, lose sight of what the woman's half is. In urging that they must have a hand in law-making and government and public life generally, they do not see that woman's peculiar work is pretty independent of laws and of government, is rather in private life. For it is just where the law cannot reach that woman is supreme. It is just in the finer, more personal and intimate relationships of life, which government cannot include, that woman finds her work waiting for her, which she alone can do—what Octavia Hill calls "the out-of-sight, silent work."

That woman is today neglecting this, her own part of the world's work, I think is everywhere apparent. Surely we do not need more laws; what we do need is more of the spirit which shall make people want to obey the laws which we have. What else does it mean when we say we cannot enforce the laws? The suffragists are clamoring for more laws, for more of the man-element in society; the anti-suffragists feel that it is the inner life and character, the mother's work, which everywhere needs strengthening. Settlement workers, doctors, ministers, and police commissioners, are beginning to feel this, too. They are telling us that in their work they find that no laws and no institutions can take the place of home teaching and influence with young people. The outer restraint and penalty are little effective unless they are met by the inner desire to do right.

On points like these I believe the accent should be laid today. The pendulum is swinging too far away from the things which our mothers and grandmothers made their chief concern. What is called "the rise of woman," her new feeling of influence and power, are blessings only as they help her to do better and of freer choice the things which are in tune with Nature and with the need of the world.

ESSAY XV

THE IMPERATIVE DEMAND UPON WOMEN IN THE HOME

MRS. CHARLES BURTON GULICK

Anne Hathaway Gulick, wife of Professor Charles B. Gulick of Harvard University; graduated at the Framingham State Normal School; taught four years in Boston and Cambridge, and is Secretary of the Public Interests' League of Massachusetts.

J. A. H.

In his address to the Associated Press on April 21, 1915, President Wilson said: "You deal in the raw material of opinion, and if my convictions have any validity, *opinion* ultimately governs the world." This is exactly what the anti-suffragists believe and teach. They know that the vote merely registers public opinion, it does not make it. Therefore, they oppose laying the useless burden of the ballot on the shoulders of woman, who already has every opportunity in her own special province to mold public opinion by educating the inmates of her home to live right and to think right. From such homes, where high principles are inculcated, comes the public spirited, right minded man, whose vote registers the fact that the mother in that home has done her duty faithfully and well. A woman who has thus fulfilled her obligation to the world knows that there is not time left to take up political duties. Either the home or the politics must suffer. In the end, in the great majority of cases, nature would assert herself, and the political duties would be neglected.

A minister, who is a suffragist, is quoted recently as saying: "Our young men, we believe, would be safer if their mothers and wives had the ballot, for they are the ones most injured by many evils." In what way will our young men be safer because their mothers and their wives have the ballot? Instead of devoting themselves wholly to teaching their sons and daughters the value of self-restraint, of respect for the rights and comfort of others, and the importance of high ideals of citizenship, if these same mothers and wives are dividing their attention between the home and political strife and strain, can they reasonably be expected to fulfill their greatest duty successfully? No woman should be obliged to divide her energies, and so have less time to give to the study of her children. No two children are alike, and each child requires special consideration and care for its best development. Can any one tell at what moment a child may need unusual attention and thought to guide it aright? Supposing the mother had the ballot, would the political campaign wait because her child was going through a particularly trying period, when a step one way or the other might make or mar its character? Or would the child wait to take the step because it was important for the mother to throw all the weight of her sound sense and good influence into the political campaign, and she must, therefore, just at this critical time set aside her home duties? No, most certainly not. The mother must have *no* other duties which could come before her home duties at any time.

Some one said recently: "A man must have a place to go from and to come to." In order to make him continue to want to go from and come to his home, there must be something there to make him look forward to the home-coming with pleasure as the reward of his labor. If this home is kept by a woman who cannot be at home often when most needed, who labors under the excitement of the political campaign, how long is he going to look forward to his home-coming? Of course, the answer to this is that most women would not spend any more time over politics than they do now. But if that is so, of what use will they be as voters, and why add a perfectly useless body of voters, when this addition to the electorate will mean an increase in the expenses of the government and consequently higher cost of living, already too high for the average family?

We do not believe with Mr. Creel that "the old fashioned idea of home is bunk," nor do we agree with Mr. Roger Sherman Hoar, who is reported as saying that "woman suffrage, by doubling the electorate, will double the opportunities of each man for political interest." He goes on to say that when a man's wife becomes a voter he will talk politics with her and will give more weight to her political opinion, thereby learning the home point of view on home matters. Is it probable that a man who has not spent enough time with his wife to know what the home point of view is before she has a vote, would be induced to spend more time there because she had? It is much more likely that he would spend less time there, since without political duties she was unable to make his home attractive, and with political duties she would have even less time to give to the making of a good home. Further on we read: "With increased interest in matters political"—this increase to be brought about by giving women the vote—"the men will scrutinize their public servants more carefully." What becomes here of the contention of the suffragists that the *ballot* is the only thing that wakens interest in good government, if the men who already have the ballot are not interested in good government, but need to have the women enfranchised before they can have a real interest in matters political?

No, woman must specialize in the home. I am not speaking of those who "by choice or accident have missed the highest privilege of womanhood," as Mr. Pyle ably puts it, but of the great majority of women. To my mind the advantages of a properly conducted home life far outweigh the advantages of any institution, no matter how good. That I am not alone in this opinion is witnessed by the fact that the trustees of the best orphan asylums are making every effort to diminish the number of children in their institutions and to place the children in homes. They have learned that even a poorly conducted home is better than a well conducted asylum, and that they have no right to deprive children of the benefits of family life. Yet the feminists, closely allied with the suffragists, advocate putting children of tender age into institutions, where, according to them, they will be better cared for than at home. "If they are well, the institution nurse is as good; if they are ill, she is much better than the mother" says one suffrage leader. Those of us who have known better can only pity people who hold such beliefs. To them mother love can have no meaning. Yet those of us who have felt this mother love, know what a guiding star it has been, and must always continue to be, brightening steadily as the years go by, and beckoning us more persistently than ever to higher ideals when it is only a memory. Who would dare deprive our children of this precious heritage? Only the unknowing.

After all, the women who rebel against the idea that home is the place for woman are largely those who misunderstand the duties of home, who think only of the drudgery, and forget to think of the happiness that comes with watching our families develop under our care. Although the mother must do all the work in the average family, it is not from these homes where in most cases the women are happily busy with their home duties that most of the agitation about abandonning the home comes, but from among those people who have too much leisure on their hands, and who, unfortunately, do not find sufficiently exciting the duties of training good citizens. Whatever our work in life, whatever our occupation, we cannot rid ourselves of drudgery. Is there not more deadening, unvarying monotony for the business woman, the shop girl, the factory hand, than for the woman in the home who is her own mistress and can in some degree regulate and vary her work to suit her own pleasure? It is only because such work is new and untried by them that many women think it preferable to home duties; but the fact that so many girls in industry marry young to get away from this uncongenial work proves that when tried it is not found either so exciting or so interesting as these advocates of woman in industry and out of the home imagine.

Do not mistake me: No woman should spend all of her time at home. Public needs and social duties must be attended to. From the latter she brings refreshment and new ideas to the home, and by giving a proper share of her energies to the former she can do her part toward helping the community in which she lives to be constantly improving itself, and so to become an ideal place in which to develop worthy citizens. With these interests she can be a real influence for good, and without them she must fall short of ideal motherhood. We must not forget that a woman can select her own time for her social duties, and they can be set aside at any time that more important matters need her attention in the home, but that she could not select her own time for political duties.

Let us remember, then, as Miss Lucy Price says, that after all, women in big business are not the successes, men can do that work as well and better than they. It is the women in the home, outnumbering all others fifteen to one (and fourteen of these do not keep a servant), who are really the great and typical women of the world.

ESSAY XVI

SUFFRAGE AND THE SEX PROBLEM

MRS. WILLIAM LOWELL PUTNAM

Mrs. William Lowell Putnam; a director of the American Association for the Study and Prevention of Infant Mortality; Chairman, Department of Public Health of Women's Municipal League of Boston, which has the following committees: Household Nursing, Prenatal and Obstetrical Care, Sanitation and Safety of Public Buildings and Conveyances, Hygiene of Occupations, Abatement of Noise, Social Hygiene and Quackery; a member of the National Child Welfare Exhibit Committee, and of the Massachusetts Committee on Unemployment of the American Section of the International Association; Chairman, Executive Committee of Massachusetts Milk Consumers' Association; Chairman of the Sub-Committee on Boston of the Special Aid Society for American Preparedness.

J. A. H.

More talk and less thought is expended on the subject of sex today than on almost anything else.

It is a hopeful sign for the future that society in general is awakening to the far-reaching importance of the relations between the sexes, and — feeling that these relations at present leave much to be desired — is offering many suggestions for the solution of this vexed problem, even though the suggestions themselves are not always calculated to obtain the desired results. The fact that throughout much of the civilized world, women outnumber men, combined with the attitude of certain women whose lives have been passed without personal experience of sexual relations has led to the suggestion that the sex problem may be simplified in the future by the development of a neuter sex which these people think they see approaching. But this seems hardly a likely solution, for asexuality must of necessity be self-destructive, and need not, therefore, occupy us long, though just now the type does seem rather self-concious. A less fanciful, though not more satisfying, solution is that of the feminist, who, in hunting for a cure, demands for men and women alike no restraint on sexual relations beyond the immediate desires of the two people most intimately concerned, while her milder sister, the suffragette, believes that women by voting can bring about in both sexes the control of human passion.

That the sexual relation interests the world is not so new a condition as we sometimes think; indeed, half unconsciously, sex has always been of paramount interest from the cradle to the grave, from the time when the child alone first nurses tenderly its doll, or in groups plays house, and at being father and mother and children. It is only the realization and open discussion of the interest which is new. Sex is the most vital thing in the world, for on it all but the lowest forms of life depend; hence the instinct of reproduction is equalled in its force by no other except, perhaps, that of self-preservation. We must think about it. Only let us think straight.

The reproductive instinct is normally stronger in men than in women; because in matters of sex, whatever he may be in other things, man is certainly the giver and woman the receiver of the gift. This fact has led to the assumption that man is, therefore, responsible for all the sins of sex, and this would undoubtedly be true were instinct and passion matters quite beyond our personal control, but they are not. The instinct of self-preservation is the most fundamental feeling that we have, and yet in the sinking of the "Titanic" and the horror of the "Lusitania," we saw this instinct controlled—how gloriously—by the highest manhood of men, not only of those from whom we should have expected the utmost consideration, but also of those who, we might have thought, had forfeited their manhood by lives of uncontrolled and sodden self-indulgence, lives full of injury to women, and to children born through them. Their manhood was not lacking when the call to protect the women and the children came in terms which they could understand. Why were they not taught to control the other fundamental instinct of life at a time when such a thing was possible? Are men responsible for the evil of their upbringing? Is it not their mothers rather, who should bear the heaviest burden of blame?

Every man is born of woman and almost every man is cared for by a woman throughout his earliest years. The Jesuits, in their wisdom, founded on much experience, have said: "Give me a child until he is seven and after that you may do what you like with him!" It is these early years that count most in a man's future. What have the mothers done in these years? Have they taught their children the laws of the transmission of life in their sacredness and their beauty, or, while willingly telling them of all the other facts of life, have they let this one, by far the most important, go untold, fear tying their tongues, and given to themselves the excuse of ignorance unequal to its task—an ignorance which in a mother is culpable—I had almost said criminal? Moreover, the responsibility of women for the moral standards of men does not end with their boyhood, for each sex is ultimately what the other demands of it to be. Men have demanded purity of their women, but women have not demanded it of men. Have not good women been in the habit of receiving into their society men whose past they know to have been bad—yes, and even of encouraging their daughters to marry such men for the sake of money or of social position? Women's responsibility for the social evil is greater than that of men, and those who are most responsible are the good women of the community. The arraignment is severe, but is it not deserved?

It is in childhood that the teaching of the sex relation must be given,—with the children that the training of self-control must begin. If men and women are started right in childhood, the later time will take care of itself. I would not belittle the father's influence, nor his teaching of his children; but of the two the mother is the more important, for the man who has talked of all things with his mother, to whom the sacredness of motherhood is indissolubly bound up with the great instinct of reproduction, will find it very hard to go far wrong. The girl, too, who understands the laws of her own nature and that of the young men whom she meets, will be in a position not only to choose her mate more wisely, but in the things that come up every day among young people of opposite sexes she will not excite in him, by word and gesture, through mere careless ignorance, as is so often done, a passion, which, though she go free and ignorant of harm, may bring to him much needless suffering, and may sometimes end in ruin both for him and for some other.

Women, through their training of their sons and daughters, hold the future of the world in their keeping. This training cannot be given by the enactment of laws; we cannot legislate the control of human passion. The law-maker bears no relation to the character builder.

> "They're no more like than hornet's nests and hives
> Or printed sarmons be to holy lives."

Law can only prevent wrongdoing, it is negative at best, for its appeal in the end must be to fear, and a people ruled by fear becomes a race of slaves. In a free country it is impossible to enforce a law unless the will of the people is behind it; and the moulding of this will, its training and development, must come in early childhood and must be done by its women. There is no greater sophistry than that women need the vote to protect themselves and one another from evil men. Were most men libertines today, no law could be enforced against them. Were all men self-controlled and pure in heart, no law would be required. The failure of the women—the good women of the community—to bring up their sons to be such men cannot be corrected by any short and easy road, nor can their responsibility for the present evil be obliterated by talk. Women have failed to do their duty, and the only way to prevent further evil is to do that duty now.

ESSAY XVII

SUFFRAGE A STEP TOWARD FEMINISM

LILY RICE FOXCROFT

Lily Rice Foxcroft, daughter of the late Rev. Dr. Charles B. Rice of Danvers, Mass., for nearly twenty years Secretary of the Congregational Board of Pastoral Supply; wife of Frank Foxcroft, editor of "The Living Age." Frequent contributor to the religious press, the author of a volume entitled, "While You Are a Girl," and a well-known speaker in opposition to woman suffrage.

J. A. H.

The strongest motive for anti-suffrage action is the deepening dread of woman suffrage as a menace to the home. The radical suffragists have little use for the home, and the radical suffragists are young and brilliant, and their following grows rapidly. It is they who are in the public eye; whom the reporters interview; who, far more than the conservatives, are really influencing the thought of the day. They claim to be the consistent thinkers, reasoning from the common premise to conclusions from which "older women" shrink. They welcome with whole-hearted enthusiasm the theory of "economic independence."

This theory was first popularized by the *Woman's Journal*, in a notable series of articles by Mrs. Charlotte Perkins Gilman, an associate editor, which appeared weekly in 1904, and of which the central thought was, "The woman should be in the home as much as the man is, no more." She urged women to "come out of their little monogamous harems," promised that "when *all* women are in industry, the conditions of industry will be compelled to suit the conditions of maternity," and predicted the time when "a man would no more think of having a woman become his house servant than a woman would think of marrying her butler and retaining him in that capacity." Mrs. Gilman summarized these ideas, again, in a lecture in New York last year: "The home of the future is one in which not one stroke of work shall be done except by professional people who are paid by the hour."

This theory meets so well the anti-suffrage argument that the woman, while spending most of her time within the home, cannot be expected to attain outside it a degree of efficiency equal to that of the man, that it naturally becomes part of the creed of the logical and consistent suffragist. Miss Henrietta Rodman—a wife who, like Miss Fola La Follette, retains her maiden name, because taking that of a husband "dwarfs individuality"—gave to a reporter of the *Boston Herald* last year her opinion that "a house is as demoralizing a place to stay in all day as a bed," and assured him that the ideal feminist apartment-house, with its co-operative nursery on the top floor, had its plans actually drawn, its site chosen. "Trained staffs are to relieve women of the four primitive industries—care of houses, clothes, food and children." "By real motherhood," said Miss Rodman, "I do not mean washing the baby's clothes, preparing its food, watching over its sleep, nursing it through its baby illnesses, nor, in later years, darning the children's stockings, making or even mending their clothes, preparing their food or supervising their education. All these things can be done better by experts."

No one can follow the utterances of this group of suffragists without noting the constant slight cast on "domestic drudgery," and the eagerness to prove other lines of activity better adapted to women. "There is rising revolt among women," wrote Miss Edna Kenton, in *The Century* for November, 1913, "against the unspeakable dullness of unvaried home life. It has been a long, deadly routine, a life-servitude imposed on her for ages in a man-made world."

General Rosalie Jones, of "hiking fame," who is now breaking into the automobile business, says: "There are idiot asylums in every state whose inmates are expert at darning and mending. Any one of those idiots sitting by the fireside could do the family mending, while the woman of education, ingenuity and common sense, could utilize her faculties to the betterment of her family and the country.... After suffrage is granted, women will no longer be content to waste their brains in this manner." Miss Inez Boissevain's "Ten Minutes-a-Day Housekeeping" is well known, as is her declaration to the reporter that she "should go crazy if she had to do housework one whole day." "Young children," she admitted, "need their mother. But," she added hopefully, "the age at which they can be left with others is much less than it was formerly supposed to be." Mrs. Rheta Childe Dorr, Mrs. Pankhurst's closest companion on her last United States tour, says: "Men are not yet used to seeing their wives in the role of wage-earners. They'll have to get used to it, that's all.... I don't say that every married woman must go to work outside her home. I should commit suicide if I had to spend my life doing housework, but some women probably like to do it. Let them do it then. All I ask is that every woman, married or single, should be allowed to choose the work in which she finds the most pleasure."

"To choose the work in which she finds the most pleasure"—there is the real individualistic note, sounded so often by the radical suffragists. It is struck still more clearly when to the reporter's question: "What about the argument that the wife with a business career is apt to deprive her husband of the joys of fatherhood?" Mrs. Dorr replies: "No one but the individual woman herself has any right to decide whether or not she shall have children. That is a question which she alone is entitled to settle."

In the same tone of contempt for the domestic round in which the average wife and mother has been accustomed to find her fair share of human satisfaction, Mrs. Susan Fitzgerald wrote in the opening number of "*Femina*": "Of course, some women don't want to do independent work; some prefer the quiet routine and detail of the home and are satisfied to make a profession of its many little refinements, even as many men have not the ambition to go into business for themselves.... But the creative artist, whether in a profession or business, gets most of the joy of living out of the satisfaction that comes to him in his work, and so I say, do away with the prejudice against married women working outside their homes."

Miss Alyse Gregory—who has campaigned for suffrage in Connecticut and New Jersey with striking success—says: "Girls should be self-supporting up to the time of their marriage, and after marriage up to the time when they begin to bear children. During the child-bearing period there might be some provision made for mothers by the State, as is now done in France; then all women who have reared families and who again find themselves with leisure on their hands, should again be self-supporting." This, of course, is the Socialist view, and Miss Gregory, like so many of the younger suffragists, is presumably a Socialist.

Another pronounced advocate of economic independence is Mrs. Havelock Ellis—an English suffragist much fêted on her visits to this country—of whom an admirer writes in the *Chicago Herald*, that "she has never accepted a penny from her husband since they were married." It will be noticed that all these women are in professional work, in which their earnings may reasonably be expected to provide "expert" care for their children. Incidentally, does not that support the anti-suffrage claim that the suffrage movement is gauged to the talents and habits of exceptional, rather than average, women, and that its principles are not those under which the average woman's life finds its best development?

This tendency away from domestic life fosters the very evils which conservative suffragists hope to remedy by the vote. Even more startling is the tone taken in the discussion of "sex problems." Interviewed on the subject of "war babies" last summer by an enterprising syndicate which spread her views all over the country, Mrs. Rheta Childe Dorr said: "There are always war babies at a time when normal restraints are removed and slackened. After a great religious revival in any town there is an increased number of illegitimate children.... The government endowed immorality when it entered the war.... The government made war, the war made war babies—then let the government take care of them."

To the same interviewer, Miss Eleanor Gates, of the Empire State Campaign Committee, said: "It's unfortunate that the parents of these babies did not take out licenses to be parents.... But more unfortunate, to my mind, than an omission of the license, is the fact that motherhood should ever be counted a crime.... And, when all is said and done, I, myself, respect the unmarried woman with a child more than I do the married woman with a poodle."

These are the utterances of conspicuous leaders of the younger, more radical wing of the woman suffrage movement; and no one who follows with any care their speeches and writings can claim that they are out of character. Is it unfair to say such utterances confuse moral values and weaken the sense of individual responsibility?

This regret that "motherhood should ever be counted a crime" is often more tersely expressed in the phrase "right to motherhood," first made fashionable, I believe, by Mr. Bernard Shaw. It was given publicity last June through an address made by Prof. W. I. Thomas of the University of Chicago at the banquet held by the Chicago Equal Suffrage Association in honor of the National Executive Council. Professor Thomas said, "in substance"—I quote the *Woman's Journal*—"that many women who could not marry were earnestly desirous of children, and that it ought to be recognized that monogamy was not the only relation in which it was respectable for a woman to have a child." The National Association, as is well known, is the conservative wing of the wrangling suffragist army, and contains most of those "middle-aged reformers" whom the "younger generation" dispose of so easily by saying that they have not kept up with the times. Miss Alice Stone Blackwell promptly combatted the speaker's opinions, and the *Woman's Journal* reports that she was heartily applauded.

But Professor Thomas is not so easily disavowed. A ten-page pamphlet, "Votes for Women," published by the Massachusetts Woman Suffrage Association, is of his authorship. In *The Case for Woman Suffrage*, a bibliography with critical comments, published by the National College Equal Suffrage League in 1913, eighty-eight lines are given to quotations from Professor Thomas's works, while Miss Blackwell's receive only forty. Such comparisons may seem trifling, but they are significant. If any one doubts the hold of the feminist ideas upon many of the most influential suffragists, he may be convinced by himself examining *The Case for Woman Suffrage*. Anti-suffragists are often accused of arguing from isolated, casual utterances. For my part, I find it impossible to reproduce, by any quotations, the impression of recklessness left by habitually reading publications, both American and English, in sympathy with suffrage.

Our age is not one that can afford to trifle with recklessness. Its own problems are of the sort that call for prudence and restraint. The International Purity Congress in San Francisco has lately drawn attention to the spread of immorality among school girls. Suffragists offer to "mother the community." It is the individual girl that needs mothering. She is not helped to self-control by reading in her favorite news-paper that Inez Haynes Gilmore, interviewed as to the use of "obey" in the marriage service, has said: "To me the promise to love and honor is more extraordinary—it's easier to promise to obey. It's impossible to promise to control the emotions." The lesson the girl draws from a play like Hindle Wakes, when Inez Milholland, in *McClure's*, calls her attention to it, is not that men must be as chaste as women, but that it is one of women's rights to be as lax as men.

Professor Thomas' views called forth resolutions from the Executive Board of the National Suffrage Association, which took a curious form. They read: "While we do not wish to criticise the speaker's remarks as such, we heard them with profound misgivings as to their effect upon the cause of suffrage in the campaign states." The anti-suffrage majorities in the campaign states certainly proved the misgivings well-timed. But, however such remarks may have been received, is it not a significant fact that they were ventured, by a reputable man, at a reputable gathering? Can anyone doubt that radical views are startlingly on the increase?

Two years ago Mrs. Winifred Harper Cooley wrote in *Harper's Weekly* of the "single standard": "There is a violent altercation going on continually, within the ranks of feminists in all countries, regarding this question. The conservative women reformers think the solution is in hauling men up to the standard of virginal purity that has always been set for women. The other branch, claiming to have a broader knowledge of human nature, asserts that it is impossible and perhaps undesirable to expect asceticism from all men and women." In the *Forum*, of April, 1915, a correspondent from California signing herself "Lottie Montgomery," expanded in revolting detail what was, after all, pretty much the same idea. "On every hand," she remarked, "we hear of the 'single standard of morals,' by which the 'purists' mean a strict monogamous life for both men and women, and by which the feminists mean an opportunity to express themselves sexually whenever they see fit without the interference and permission of the Church and State, and this neither constitutes promiscuity, nor yet polyandry, but an opportunity to live your own life in your own way and not to have to sacrifice your name, privacy, self-respect and income in order to gratify the sex instinct." And, passing from theory to practical observation, she asserts: "Whether we like to admit it or not, the fact remains that women today, from the mansion to the tenement, are acquiring sex experience outside of marriage, which accounts for the great mental strides they have made with the past two decades." In the publication, by a leading editor, of such sentiments, we have an alarming sign of the times.

There are too many such signs. Do we not all know long-established magazines which have published, within the last five years, serials that they would not have considered fifteen years ago?

Says *Punch's* reviewer of a recent heroine: "Her point of view was typified in her attitude toward the illicit and incidental motherhood of one of her acquaintances. Without hearing the facts, she pronounced it to be 'a courageous stand against conventional morality,' which it just possibly might have proved to be upon enquiry, and by no means a weak surrender to immediate desires, as much more probably it was in fact." The author of *Angela's Business* depicts precisely the same mental attitude in the crimson-faced woman at the Redmantle Club, who demands of Charles in an angry sort of way, "Don't you favor a public reception immediately to splendid Flora Travenna? Don't you think she's struck a great blow for freedom?" — Flora Trevenna having just returned home after an absence of two years in the company of another woman's husband.

One of Robert Herrick's heroines prophesies — in line with Professor Thomas — "The time will come when single women like me, who work as men work, will have the courage to love and bear children if they need — and men will respect them."

Will it be believed that an English magazine of fine literary quality, in which the work of Galsworthy and Arnold Bennett has often appeared, has printed an article by a woman pleading for a public sentiment in favor of irregular unions? "Women will go a step further toward freedom than men have dared to go," says Mrs. Walter Gallachan. "I believe that if there were some open recognition of these partnerships outside of marriage, not necessarily permanent, there would be many women who would be willing to undertake such unions gladly; there would even be some women, as I believe, who would prefer them to the present system that binds them permanently to one partner for life."

To many women these views seem so shocking that they cannot believe them to be widespread. I can only say that such women are leading "sheltered lives." Said a conspicuous young feminist in an interview given to a Boston Sunday paper, "It is both cruel and foolish (eugenically and ethically) to prevent people from trying more than once to find their ideal comrade for race propagation." The fiction of today is full of the disgusting experiences of young persons trying to find their ideal comrades. And an appalling number of these books bear marks of brilliant talent, utterly unconscious of moral standards, "studies of adolescence," many of them are. Illicit relations are entered on in the most casual way and dropped as casually, and yet glorified as marking new eras of "development."

I know, of course, the answer made by thoughtful, conscientious suffragists who believe as strongly as I do in the integrity of the home, when facts like these are brought to their attention. "All suffragists are not feminists. All feminism is not of this extreme sort. Feminism is nothing but a theory, anyway."

Each of us must judge from her own observation; but it should be observation, not merely of the lives of one's personal acquaintance, but of current thought and tendency. Many of us are convinced that an increasing and influential number of suffragists are feminists, that a great deal of feminism is of this extreme sort, and that it is a "theory" which, through channels direct and indirect, is poisoning our literature and our social life.

IMPORTANT ANTI-SUFFRAGE PUBLICA-TIONS

(For pamphlets and leaflets on the various aspects of the question address the Secretary of the Women's Anti-Suffrage Association, Kensington Building. 687 Boylston Street, Boston.)

BOOKS AND PAMPHLETS

James M. Buckley, THE WRONG AND PERIL OF WOMAN SUFFRAGE. (Fleming H. Revell Co., New York.) Not a recent book, but contains a good deal of permanently useful matter not found elsewhere.

Helen Kendrick Johnson, WOMAN AND THE REPUBLIC. (25c; The Woman's Protest, 237 West 39th Street. New York.) Especially valuable for its information about the history of woman suffrage in relation to the political and social development of the nineteenth century.

Ida M. Tarbell, THE BUSINESS OF BEING A WOMAN. ($1.25; The Macmillan Company, New York.) The book which best expresses the anti-suffrage view of woman's place in modern society. See also Miss Tarbell's THE WAYS OF WOMAN; (The Macmillan Company,) and THE BOOK OF WOMAN'S POWER. ($1.25; do).

J. Lionel Tayler, THE NATURE OF WOMAN. ($1.25; E. P. Dutton & Company, N. Y.) The best treatment of biology and sex in their relation to the question.

E. S. Martin, THE UNREST OF WOMEN. (D. Appleton & Company, New York.) A good-natured, but shrewd, analysis of manifestations of feminism in Miss Thomas, Mrs. Belmont, Miss Millholland, etc., by the genial editor of *Life*.

Ernest Bernbaum and *George R. Conroy*, THE CASE AGAINST WOMAN SUFFRAGE, (Anti-Suffrage Association, 687 Boylston Street, Boston.) This pamphlet of fifty small pages, which briefly covers all the chief points of the anti-suffrage case, was widely distributed during the 1915 campaign.

PERIODICALS

ANTI-SUFFRAGE NOTES. Issued every other week, sometimes weekly; $1 a year. (Subscriptions should be sent to Mrs. George Sheffield, 33

Brewster Street, Cambridge.)

The Woman's Protest. Monthly. The organ of the National Association Opposed to Woman Suffrage. $1 a year. (37 West 39th Street, New York City.)

The Remonstrance. Quarterly. The organ of the Massachusetts Anti-Suffrage Association. 25c a year. (Mrs. James M. Codman, Walnut Street, Brookline.)

Lector House believes that a society develops through a two-fold approach of continuous learning and adaptation, which is derived from the study of classic literary works spread across the historic timeline of literature records. Therefore, we aim at reviving, repairing and redeveloping all those inaccessible or damaged but historically as well as culturally important literature across subjects so that the future generations may have an opportunity to study and learn from past works to embark upon a journey of creating a better future.

This book is a result of an effort made by Lector House towards making a contribution to the preservation and repair of original ancient works which might hold historical significance to the approach of continuous learning across subjects.

HAPPY READING & LEARNING!

LECTOR HOUSE LLP
E-MAIL: lectorpublishing@gmail.com